PIZZA SCHOOL

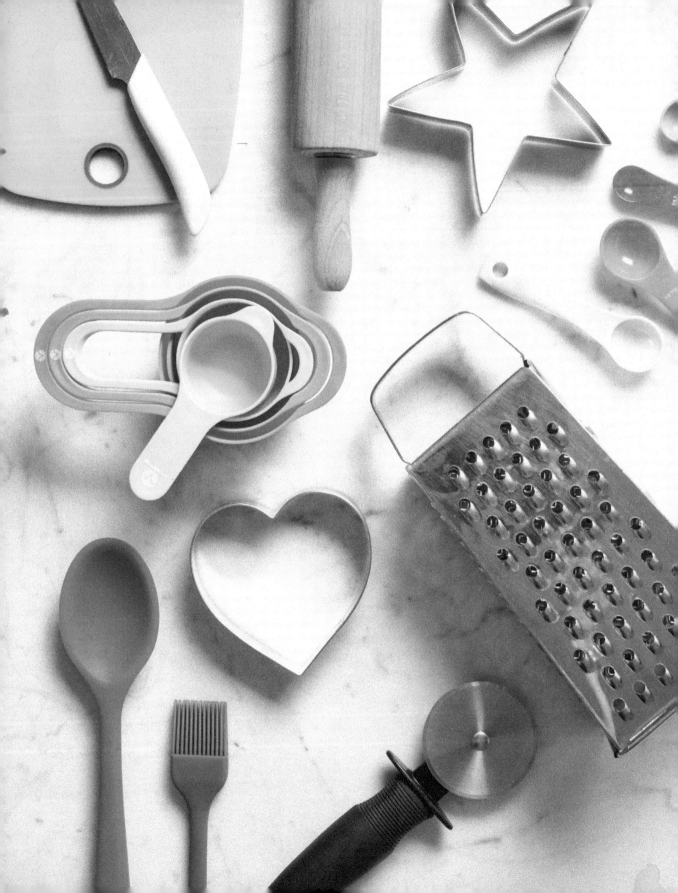

*to Ava
Merry Christmas from
your cousin
Charity!*

PIZZA SCHOOL

A Kids' Cookbook for Aspiring Pizza Makers

Charity Curley Mathews

Photography by Evi Abeler

**ROCKRIDGE
PRESS**

For general information on our other products and services or to obtain technical support, please contact our Customer Care Department within the United States at (866) 744-2665, or outside the United States at (510) 253-0500.

Rockridge Press publishes its books in a variety of electronic and print formats. Some content that appears in print may not be available in electronic books, and vice versa.

TRADEMARKS: Rockridge Press and the Rockridge Press logo are trademarks or registered trademarks of Callisto Media Inc. and/or its affiliates, in the United States and other countries, and may not be used without written permission. All other trademarks are the property of their respective owners. Rockridge Press is not associated with any product or vendor mentioned in this book.

Interior and Cover Designer: Darren Samuel
Art Producer: Maura Boland
Editor: Lauren Ladoceour and Rachel Feldman
Production Manager: Martin Worthington
Production Editor: Melissa Edeburn

Photography Evi Abeler © 2019.
Food styling by Albane Sharrar.

Author photo courtesy of ©Laura Wessell.

ISBN: Print 978-1-64152-754-5
Ebook 978-1-64152-755-2
R0

To Paul, who brought us to Italy in the first place, and our bambini who joined us along the way, Phoebe, Estelle, George, and Violet.

CONTENTS

WELCOME TO PIZZA SCHOOL!

Here it is, your very own cookbook devoted to the best food ever . . . pizza! Now you get to pick your own sauce, toppings, and even the shape of your dough. That's the magic of cooking: You decide exactly what you eat.

You'll find 26 simple recipes for everything from a traditional pizza crust to cornmeal and gluten-free options. And toppings? We've thought of everything! Cheese, olives, pepperoni, sausage (of course!), and lots more. Plus, we have tons of new ideas you'll want to try. For example, shapes: Have you ever made a star-shaped pizza? That's just the beginning of the fun you're about to have.

Every pizza is designed with you in mind, whether you're a pizza expert or you're about to make your first pie today. Each recipe has symbols showing you which skills you'll be practicing, such as using a knife or using the stovetop. When you see a STOP in a recipe, that means you'll need an adult to help you with that step. Otherwise, you're the cook in charge. Ready to get started? Let's make pizza!

A NOTE TO GROWN-UP PIZZA MAKERS

Three of my four young kids were born in Italy, where people take family and food—including pizza—very seriously.

Our kids have become cooks. I love what they're learning every time they're in the kitchen: patience, perseverance, and even compassion when it's someone else's turn to get dinner on the table. Once they started making pizza at home, the worlds of learning and eating collided in the very best way.

In this book, we're cooking from scratch and using whole foods whenever possible. Pizza can be full of fresh ingredients. Cooking from scratch with whole foods is a habit that will serve kids well for a lifetime.

Each of the 26 recipes in this book has been designed for (and tested by) kids. Your little pizza chefs will learn skills like kneading dough (and knowing when it's ready for the next step), using a food processor, cooking on a stovetop, and cutting with a kid-safe knife. They'll also tackle measuring and timekeeping, plus simple techniques for whipping up homemade sauces, like fresh tomato and pesto.

Pizza is the perfect food for kids because it's entirely customizable, especially for those with allergies. You can make dough gluten free and swap any cheese for a dairy-free option. You can omit nuts or swap them for seeds. You can choose vegetarian proteins instead of meat (or skip the protein altogether).

We've included three recipes for dough (a simple dough, a deep dish dough, and a gluten-free dough). All of the recipes in the book use one of these dough recipes. Most of the pizza recipes make two 13-inch pizzas though some recipes call only for enough ingredients to make one pizza, in which case you can either double the ingredients for toppings or freeze half the dough for future use.

I know from experience that cooking with kids can be tricky, so set the tone for a fun activity with as little stress as possible. Here's my advice on making it happen:

- From the moment you show them this book, lots of kids will want to start "Right now!" Have a plan in mind for when they'll host their first Pizza Night.

- We have one quickie crust recipe, but for the others in this book you'll want to explain that the dough needs to rise for about 30 minutes, and plan accordingly.

- Before you get started, read through the chosen recipe from start to finish and make a note of any **STOP** . These signs mean an adult should help the child with that step. By reading the recipe before starting, you'll also get an idea of which tasks your children will be able to do on their own.

- When you're ready to make pizza, help your chefs set up their workspace, complete with all the ingredients and tools needed for their chosen pizza.

- Explain your guidelines for cleaning as you go, using the oven (for example, will you push the oven buttons or will they?), measuring, and so on.

- I like to start every cooking project with a garbage bowl at hand, plus a wet rag to wipe sticky fingers, and an understanding that when I say "Hands up!" that means all little hands go straight in the air. It's helpful for safety (and sanity).

- Don't forget about the cleanup! From putting ingredients away to loading the dishwasher and wiping the counter, it's easier to set expectations at the beginning of a project instead of at the end.

- Never worry about "mistakes." These recipes are forgiving, and even if the results are lopsided or a little too crispy, trust me when I say, every kid still loves pizza. Especially a pie they made themselves.

The next time your kids beg for Pizza Night, help them pick out a recipe to make together. One day, you might find them making it for you on their own!

1

A KID'S PIZZERIA

Making your own pizza is easier than you think, but you'll want to master a few skills and techniques to make the perfect pie. From safety rules to pizza tips, you'll find what you need right here.

Pizza in 4, 3, 2, 1!

There are only four steps to making a pizza—and each one is very important. Here's how it's done:

1. **TOSS:** Make pizza dough from scratch, let it rise if it needs to, and form the dough into a round shape.

2. **SAUCE:** Make a sauce. Traditional pizza sauce is full of tomatoes, but you can use anything from pesto to barbecue sauce.

3. **TOP:** Sprinkle your favorite toppings over the sauce. Cheese, pepperoni, chicken—the choices are up to you.

4. **BAKE:** Bake the pie in a very hot oven. In a short time, you'll have a crispy crust with yummy flavors on top.

Start Here

It's fun to make your own pizza, but nothing ruins a pizza party like a major injury. Because you'll be working with graters, knives, and a screaming hot oven, follow these kitchen rules:

1. **ALWAYS COOK WITH AN ADULT.** These recipes are specially developed for kids to enjoy making, but you always need an adult around to help. When you see this symbol: **STOP**, it means stop and ask an adult to help. Usually this step involves the oven, but it also includes any task that could be dangerous to do on your own.

2. **USE TOOLS SAFELY.** Some recipes use tools like knives or graters. These tools are important, but they can be dangerous. There's nothing worse than not being able to finish making your pizza because you got hurt. Again, always cook with an adult. For older kids who are ready to start using sharper tools under supervision, see chapter 4 (page 39) for instructions on chopping safely.

3. **WASH YOUR HANDS.** Clean hands are the most useful tool in the kitchen! Wash your hands with soap and warm water, and don't rush. Make sure your hands are truly clean by singing the A-B-C song while you scrub. When the song's over, your hands should be ready to dry with a clean towel.

4. **HANDLE EGGS SAFELY.** Refrigerated eggs can be left on the counter for up to 2 hours. Bringing them up to room temperature can help the dough-making process, but it's not required for the recipes in this book, so skip it if it makes you uncomfortable. Always wash your hands with hot, soapy water after handling raw eggs.

5. **HANDLE MEAT SAFELY.** Always wash your hands with hot, soapy water before and after handling raw meat, such as the bacon, chicken, sausage, or ground beef used in these recipes. Keep all meat juices away from other raw foods, and never put any food or utensils on a cutting board that held any kind of raw meat unless the board has first been well cleaned with hot, soapy water.

6. **RINSE PRODUCE.** Give any fresh vegetables and fruits a rinse before slicing or assembling on a pizza.

7. **PREPARE YOUR WORK AREA.** Before starting any pizza project, set up all the ingredients you'll need on a clean, flat work surface. Get your measuring cups and spoons ready, grab a bowl, and make sure the pan you need is close at hand.

8. **CLEAN AS YOU GO.** Keep a wet rag and a garbage bowl on the counter. Wipe up any spills as they happen and between steps as needed. Cleaning as you go will save you a lot of time with cleanup at the end.

9. **USE POT HOLDERS.** The oven is hot, hot, *hot*. When putting pans in and out of the oven, *always* ask an adult for help.

Ingredients to Have

Combining pizza ingredients in unique ways is fun. As a pizza chef, here are the most common ingredients you'll use:

- **In the pantry:** canned beans, canned tomatoes, cornmeal, flour (all-purpose and gluten free), olive oil, olives, salt, spices, sugar, yeast (either active dry yeast or instant rise yeast; both come in ¼-ounce packages)

- **In the refrigerator:** cheeses, eggs, fresh herbs, fruits, meats, mushrooms, vegetables

- **On the counter:** garlic, nuts, onions, tomatoes

Tools to Gather

You'll need the right tools to make your pizzas. Here's the equipment you'll use:

Tools + Utensils

 CUTTING BOARD: Wooden or plastic surface used for chopping, rolling, or cutting food.

 DRY MEASURING CUPS: Used for measuring dry ingredients such as flour. They usually come in a set of standard measures, such as 1 cup, ½ cup, and so on. Handles make scooping easier.

 GRATER: Box-shaped tool made out of metal, with a handle on top and small holes on the sides. Most often used for grating cheese.

 KID-SAFE KNIFE: Child's knife with a sharp serrated blade that can chop but not slice. Typically made out of silicone with a blunt rounded end, which makes these knives safer than regular stainless-steel knives.

 MEASURING SPOONS: Used for measuring wet ingredients such as milk or oil. Usually made of glass or clear plastic so you can see the contents and measure accurately.

MIXING BOWLS: Made of plastic, ceramic, or metal. One large and one small mixing bowl should do the trick.

 PARCHMENT PAPER: A heat-resistant paper for covering baking sheets to prevent sticking.

 PASTRY BRUSH: Cooking utensil that looks like a paintbrush, used to spread oil or other liquid on food.

 PIZZA CUTTER: Knife with a long handle and round blade that rolls.

 ROLLING PIN: A long cylindrical utensil used to flatten dough.

 SCISSORS: A hand-held tool with two bypassing blades, used to cut.

SPATULA: Tool with a long handle and flat surface, used for flipping.

 WHISK: A stirring tool that helps mix air into wet ingredients.

 ZESTER: A long, metal, handheld tool with a handle at one end and small holes on one side. Often used for grating hard cheeses (such as Parmesan) or lemon rinds.

Cookware + Bakeware

 BAKING SHEET: A flat metal pan used in the oven. Also called a "cookie sheet" or "half-sheet pan." These take up a whole rack in most ovens.

 CAST IRON SKILLET: A heavy black pan with a shallow round design and a handle. Can be used on the stovetop or in an oven.

 PIZZA PAN OR STONE: A pizza pan is a flat, round metal pan with a small raised edge, while a pizza stone is a flat stone or ceramic base. Either can be used to bake pizzas in the oven.

Appliances

 BLENDER: A machine with blades and a glass jug and lid. It can be used at various speeds to chop, combine, and create smooth sauces.

 FOOD PROCESSOR: A machine that often has interchangeable blades. Used to chop ingredients into different sizes and combine into pastes or chunky sauces.

 STAND MIXER: A heavy appliance with a bowl and arm with interchangeable parts for whisking, blending, or mixing. Used to make pizza dough.

CRAFTY CUP

How much flour fits inside a measuring cup? This quick project will help you understand how important it is to measure correctly in order to get the results you want.

What you'll need: piece of paper, pencil, scissors, tape, measuring cup, flour, table knife

Step 1: Use a separate piece of paper to trace the shape on the next page.

Step 2: Cut along everything except the dotted lines.

Step 3: Fold all four sides.

Step 4: Use tape to secure the tabs. Now you have a cup.

Step 5: Next, fill the regular measuring cup from the kitchen with flour. Use the flat end of a table knife to scrape the flour from the top so the flour is level and the cup is full. Pour the flour into your square paper cup. Does your cup hold the same amount?

Now try comparing your cup of flour with other objects. See which is bigger, a cup of flour or a

- coffee mug

- baseball

- folded washcloth

- bar of soap

Which one comes the closest to a real measuring cup?

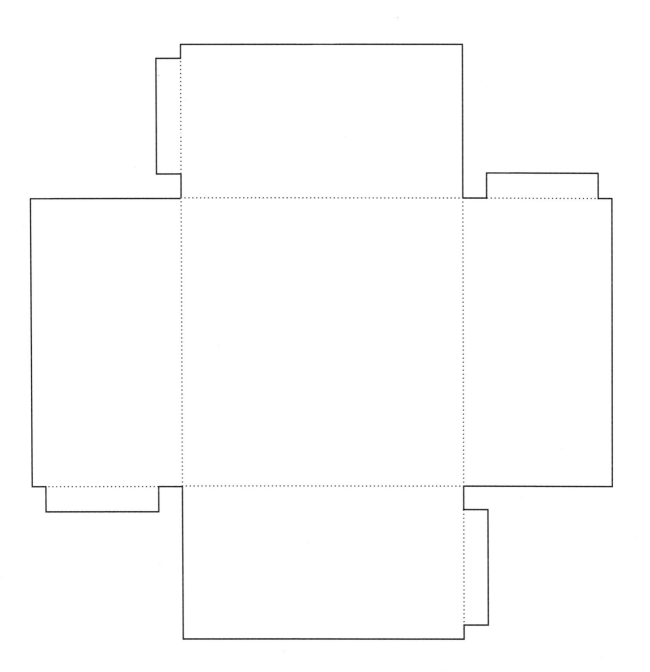

Using Tools Safely

With certain tools, it takes time to develop the skills and the confidence you need to work on your own. Nothing is more discouraging to a new baker than getting hurt, so don't be shy about asking for help from an adult. Here are two of the sorts of tools you'll be using for the recipes in this book:

Knives

Chopping and slicing are typically the first skills cooks learn. Follow these guidelines to keep your fingers safe:

- Always use a plastic child-safe knife or small chef's knife.

- When chopping, curl the tips of your fingers under in a "C" shape (like a claw) to protect them.

- Pay attention to what you are cutting. Don't get distracted.

- Use a cutting board. If the board is slipping, set it on top of a damp kitchen towel.

- When cutting, position fruits or vegetables so the flat sides are down.

- Take your time. Never rush through the process of slicing or chopping.

Graters and Microplanes

To shred or zest an ingredient, use a box grater or Microplane (which is a very fine kitchen grater with many tiny sharp blades). Be careful—it's easy to cut yourself, so follow these guidelines:

- Position the box grater or Microplane over a cutting board.

- To zest citrus (lemons, limes, oranges, etc.), wash the fruit first, then rub the rind (the skin) against the Microplane or the smallest holes on the box grater.

- To shred other fruits or vegetables, use the largest holes on a box grater.

- Always stop shredding when your fingers start to get close to the grater. Ask an adult to finish up.

Using Appliances Safely

You might use a pan on the stovetop to melt ingredients like butter or chocolate, or to prep sauces and glazes for your pizza. And you'll definitely use an oven to bake your delicious pizzas. These guidelines will help keep you from getting burned:

Using the Oven

The oven is your main tool in pizza making. It gets very hot, so you'll need to be careful when using it. These guidelines will help you keep from getting burned:

PREHEATING: Most recipes will ask you to turn on the oven as the first step. This is so the oven can reach the right temperature by the time you're ready to put your pizza in.

BAKING: Generally speaking, this means cooking a dish in the oven, instead of on the stovetop with a burner.

BROILING: Most ovens have a broiler. This is a very powerful heater at the top that's used to cook things directly under the heat source.

TRAPPING THE HEAT: Try not to open the oven door more often than you need to. Every time you do, you let heat escape that could be used to cook your dish quickly and evenly.

AVOID BANGING WHILE BAKING: Slamming doors or other loud noises can cause some dishes to collapse because the bang can knock out air that would otherwise keep your food puffy.

Pizza Maker Tips

Using a recipe takes two types of skill: science and art. Following the directions is the science part. Adding your own flourish? That's the art. Here's how to get the best results every time.

1. **READ THE RECIPE AND LOOK FOR THE SPECIAL TOOLS AND EQUIPMENT SYMBOLS:** Each recipe includes symbols to let you know if there are more advanced tools and equipment that might require an adult. Here are the symbols that you'll see throughout the book:

FOOD PROCESSOR: Chop or combine ingredients quickly using this tool's powerful motor and extra-sharp blade.

 KNIFE: When slicing anything, always use a clean cutting board and tuck your fingers under like a claw. Kid-safe knives or crinkle cutters are advised for young or beginner cooks.

 GRATER: Use one hand to steady the grater and the other to rub your ingredient against the sharp holes. (Always stop shredding when your fingers start to get close to the grater. Ask an adult to finish up.)

 STOVETOP: Some sauces and toppings require cooking in a pan before adding to your pizza.

2. **MAKE SURE YOU HAVE ALL THE INGREDIENTS YOU'LL NEED:** Before you start a recipe, make sure you've got all the ingredients. If not, ask an adult to pick up what you need from the store and make a plan for when you'll cook your pizza in the future.

3. **GET OUT ALL THE INGREDIENTS AND TOOLS:** Before starting any recipe (pizza or not), set everything you'll need on the counter. The French call this process *mise en place* (pronounced meez-on-plass), which means "everything in its place."

4. **FOLLOW THE RECIPE STEPS IN ORDER:** The steps of a recipe are written in the order they should be done. Usually there's chemistry at work. For example, if you add the flour too early, you might overwork it and end up with tough dough. Or, if you don't put the yeast in with the sugar, the dough may not rise. Follow each step as it's written.

5. **MEASURE CAREFULLY:** To correctly measure flour, always fluff up the flour with a spoon before scooping it up with your measuring cup. Then scrape across the top of the cup with the back of a knife. To get accurate measurements for liquid, use a glass measuring cup and bend down so you're eye level with the lines on the cup to see that the liquid is at the level you want.

6. **WATCH THE CLOCK:** Always remember to set a timer. When a recipe gives you a range of minutes, set your timer for the shortest time given and start checking the oven when the timer first sounds. For example, if the recipe says 10 to 12 minutes, set the timer for 10 minutes and start checking the pizza then.

7. **REMEMBER THAT RECIPES ARE GUIDELINES:** I promised a little artwork and here it is: It's okay if your final result doesn't look exactly like the picture or if you taste it and decide it needs a little salt (or something else). As long as you think your pizza is delicious, so will everyone else. You can make notes about what you want to do differently next time. This is your book, so you get to fill it with your own ideas.

2

DOUGH CLASS

Thin crust, deep dish, even gluten free . . . every pizza dough starts with one magical ingredient: yeast. Yeast are microscopic organisms that grow when you feed them. That's why the recipes you'll find in this book always include warm water and a little sugar. This combination creates the perfect setting for yeast to grow—and when they grow, your pizza dough rises.

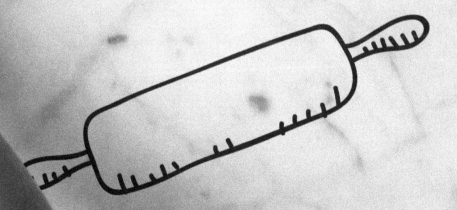

Water Temperature

The perfect temperature for making dough is between 105°F and 130°F, depending on the recipe. (Super Simple Pizza Dough, see page 20, requires water between 105°F and 110°F, whereas Cornmeal Pizza Dough (see page 24) needs hotter water: 120°F to 130°F.) At the right temperature, yeast dissolves, allowing it to become active and stay active once you add the rest of the ingredients.

Heat the water in a microwave-safe measuring cup for 30 seconds at a time, run water from the faucet until it's hot, or use a kettle to warm the water and pour it into a liquid measuring cup. To make sure the water temperature is correct for the recipe, place the tip of a thermometer into your measuring cup. Too cold? Pour out a little water and add more hot water. Too hot? Pour out a little water and add cold tap water.

Measuring

Baking dough is a science. Chemical reactions are happening when you put a pizza inside your hot oven! To get the best results from these chemical reactions, the measurements of your ingredients need to be accurate. Many professional bakers use a digital scale to weigh their ingredients because it's the most precise way. But because we're beginner pizza makers, we're going to start with measuring cups—and a few tricks:

- **MEASURE FLOUR IN A METAL OR PLASTIC MEASURING CUP:** The most accurate way to measure flour involves three steps: (1) fluff up the flour with a spoon, (2) fill the measuring cup, and (3) scrape the extra flour off the top of the cup with the back of a kitchen knife. If you just scoop the flour straight from the container, you'll end up with too much flour, and the dough will be dense and thick instead of light and fluffy.

- **MEASURE LIQUID IN A GLASS MEASURING CUP THAT LOOKS LIKE A SMALL PITCHER:** Once you've filled the measuring cup, bend down so you can see the highest part of the liquid at eye level. Look at the slight dip in the middle of the cup; that's the point you want to measure. If the dip is at the right measurement for your recipe, you're all set. If not, add a little more or pour a little out and measure again.

Kneading

By pushing, folding, and twisting dough, you can shape it into a smooth ball that's perfect for pizza. Proper kneading takes five to eight minutes. Here's how to do it:

1. **PREPARE A CLEAN, FLAT SURFACE:** Clear a countertop or large cutting board, and stand on a stool if necessary so the work surface is at your waist.

2. **COMBINE THE INGREDIENTS FOR THE DOUGH:** Follow the recipe, combining the flour, yeast, salt, water, and oil. When the dough becomes too thick to stir with a wooden spoon, it's ready to knead.

3. **TRANSFER THE DOUGH TO THE WORK SURFACE:** Sprinkle ¼ cup of flour onto the work surface and place the dough on top. The dough should be a loose, sticky lump.

4. **GATHER THE DOUGH INTO A PILE:** Dust your hands with flour then plunge the heel of your hand into the center of the lump. Fold the dough into a ball, then plunge the heel of your hand in again. If the dough doesn't start losing its stickiness quickly, sprinkle another handful of flour on top and work it in.

5. **PUNCH THE DOUGH:** Giving the dough a good punch activates the gluten (gluten is what makes dough soft and chewy); then press, fold, twist, and repeat.

6. **STOP!** Stop kneading when the dough is shiny and smooth. Test: Pick up the ball of dough and drop it onto the counter. Does it hold its shape? Perfect!

Rising

Most pizza doughs need an hour or two to rise. But because most of you are beginner bakers, we've included doughs that don't take so long to rise. The Super Simple Pizza Dough (page 20) doesn't require rising at all, and the other two only need 30 or fewer minutes of rising time. So when you're ready for the dough to rise, here's how to do it: You'll add a bit of olive oil to a big bowl and rub it all over the inside of the bowl with clean hands. This will stop the rising dough from sticking to the bowl (if the dough sticks it won't be able to rise as high). Place a damp towel over the top (just a little wet and definitely not dripping), then position the bowl in a warm spot, such as on a table next to a sunny window.

DID YOU KNOW?

Yeast is alive! But don't worry, it can't bite. In fact, the tiny pellets of yeast you see in a package from the store are actually "dormant." That means the yeast is sleeping. Warm water is the special ingredient that wakes it up.

Once it's awake, what happens? The yeast begins feeding on the sugar in the dough and releases a compound you've maybe heard of at school: carbon dioxide (CO_2). It's all those tiny CO_2 bubbles that slowly create the rising effect in dough.

Rolling + Shaping

This step comes after the pizza dough has risen, or right after kneading if the dough doesn't require rising. The recipes in this book will guide you through two versions:

Traditional Method

This method is a bit more authentic and fun! You'll sprinkle some cornmeal on your surface and then get to shaping.

1. **SPRINKLE CORNMEAL ON YOUR WORKSPACE:** Sprinkle a little cornmeal (or drizzle a bit of olive oil) on your counter or cutting board.

2. **PRESS THE PIZZA DOUGH:** Flatten the dough ball into a round disc. Then use your middle three fingers to press the dough out, starting from the center, widening that disc into a large circle (about 6 inches across and ½-inch thick). Don't worry if it's not perfectly round yet.

3. **STRETCH THE DOUGH:** Some pizza chefs in restaurants toss dough in the air to stretch it. This looks pretty cool, but at home it's better to carefully pick up the dough with both hands on one edge, letting the rest of the dough hang down. Let gravity help the dough stretch while you gently turn the dough like a wheel, going in one direction. Slowly pull the dough from hand to hand. Stretch the dough until it's about 13 inches across. Don't worry if there are some thin spots or holes. We'll fix them next.

4. **MOVE THE DOUGH TO THE PAN:** This is a good time to line the pan or baking sheet with parchment paper or sprinkle it with a handful of cornmeal. Carefully scoot the pizza dough onto the prepared pan or baking sheet. Then take a look: Is the dough about 13 inches across? Are there any holes? Press any thick edges to flatten them out, or pinch dough together to patch holes and thin spots. You want a mostly flat circle. No worries if the edges aren't higher than the center. The toppings will weigh the middle of the dough down, allowing the edges to puff up naturally.

Simplified Method

This method uses parchment paper for the easiest cleanup possible.

1. **HAVE TWO PIECES OF PARCHMENT PAPER READY:** Use a pastry brush to coat the first piece of parchment paper with olive oil.

2. **ROLL TO FLATTEN:** Place the pizza dough on top of the parchment paper and use a rolling pin to flatten it into a 13-inch circle.

3. **TRANSFER TO THE PAN:** Use the edges of the parchment paper as handles to lift the dough onto the pizza pan.

And if you don't have time or just don't want to experiment with making pizza dough yet, don't worry! You can find ready-made pizza dough at the grocery store that will taste great. Skip ahead to Sauce Class (page 29) for ideas on topping any dough deliciously.

SUPER SIMPLE PIZZA DOUGH

I never would've guessed how simple it was to make my own pizza dough—until I mastered this recipe! You won't even have to wait for the dough to rise. You'll find tons of ideas for toppings in the following chapters.

2¼ cups **all-purpose flour,** divided

1 package (2¼ teaspoons) **instant rise yeast**

1 teaspoon **sugar**

1 teaspoon **salt**

⅔ cup very warm **water** (105°F to 110°F)

3 tablespoons **extra-virgin olive oil**

1. **Preheat the oven.** If you're baking the pizza now, check the recipe to find out how hot the oven needs to be. Most pizzas in this book will require an oven temperature of 425°F to 450°F.

2. **Wake up the yeast.** In a large bowl, combine 1 cup of flour, the yeast, sugar, and salt. Use a kitchen thermometer to measure the water temperature; add more hot or cold water as needed until the temperature reaches between 105°F and 110°F. Then add the water and olive oil. Mix with a rubber spatula or wooden spoon until well blended, about 1 minute.

3. **Make the dough.** Slowly add 1 more cup of flour to make a soft, dry dough. Use your hands to pull the dough together into a ball.

4. **Knead the dough.** Sprinkle a handful of the remaining ¼ cup of flour on a clean cutting board or counter. Add a little more flour to your hands and knead until the dough changes from sticky to smooth, 5 to 8 minutes. (Want more details? See page 17 for more kneading instructions.)

5. **Shape or store for later.** To store the dough for later, shape it into two balls. Wrap them in plastic wrap or place them in covered bowls in the refrigerator for up to three days, or in the freezer for up to one month. Ready to make pizza now? See pages 18 to 19 for instructions on rolling out the dough, then get ideas for toppings from the recipes in chapters 5 to 8.

Did You Know?

There are two kinds of yeast most bakers use at home: active dry yeast and instant rise yeast. Active dry yeast must be dissolved in water, while instant rise yeast can be added straight to the dough.

For Laughs!

Why did the man go into the pizza business?
He wanted to make some dough.

CORNMEAL PIZZA DOUGH

PREP TIME: 50 minutes
COOK TIME: 40 minutes
MAKES: 2 (11- to 13-inch) pizzas

TOOLS TO GATHER

1 large mixing bowl

Measuring spoons and cups

Kitchen thermometer

Wooden spoon or rubber spatula

Cutting board or clean counter space

Plastic wrap or clean kitchen towel

2 cast iron skillets

HINT

It's all about using a skillet, so be sure to have an adult close by to help get the skillet in and out of the oven—skillets are heavy!

Perfect for Chicago-style deep dish pizza, this thick and hearty pizza dough is sturdy enough to hold a pile of toppings.

3½ cups **all-purpose flour**, divided, plus more for dusting

¼ cup **cornmeal**

1 package (2¼ teaspoons) **instant rise yeast**

1 tablespoon **sugar**

1½ teaspoons **salt**

1 cup very warm **water** (120°F to 130°F)

⅓ cup **extra-virgin olive oil**

1. **Combine the dry ingredients.** In a large bowl, combine 1½ cups of flour (save the rest for step 3), the cornmeal, yeast, sugar, and salt. Stir until everything is combined.

2. **Add the warm water.** Use a kitchen thermometer to measure the water temperature, adding more hot or cold water as needed until the temperature reaches between 120°F and 130°F. Carefully drizzle the water into the bowl with the dry ingredients and stir. The mixture should look like a thick paste.

3. **Add the rest of the flour.** Pour in the remaining 2 cups of flour and stir with a wooden spoon or rubber spatula until the dough becomes stiff.

4. **Knead the dough.** Sprinkle a handful of flour onto a clean cutting board or counter. Flip the bowl of dough onto the cutting board. Knead the dough with the heels of your hands until it changes from sticky to smooth, 5 to 8 minutes.

5. **Let the dough rise.** Rinse out the used mixing bowl and dry it. Pour about 1 tablespoon of olive oil into the bowl and use clean hands to rub the oil all over. Place the dough in the bowl and cover the bowl with plastic wrap or a clean kitchen towel. Set the bowl in a warm place (for example, on a sunny windowsill) and allow the dough to rise until it has doubled in size (about 30 minutes).

6. **Punch the dough.** When the dough has risen, use your fists to flatten it down in the bowl. Then divide the dough in half.

7. **Store or bake.** To store the dough for later, shape it into two balls and wrap them individually in plastic or place them in covered bowls in the refrigerator for up to three days, or freeze for up to one month. Ready to bake? Press the dough into the bottom and up the sides of two skillets (or use one skillet at a time, storing the extra dough in the refrigerator while you wait). Then add your toppings. See chapters 5 to 8 for ideas. Cover and bake at 450°F on the middle rack for 25 minutes. When the cheese has melted and the crust looks golden, use a spatula to free the side of the crust from the skillet. Peek to check the bottom of the crust. Does it look golden, too? If not, bake the pizza on the bottom rack for 2 minutes longer.

For Laughs!

What do you call a sleeping pizza? *A piZZZZZZa.*

GLUTEN-FREE PIZZA DOUGH

PREP TIME: 25 minutes, plus 15 minutes rest
COOK TIME: 20 minutes
MAKES: 1 (9- to 12-inch) pizza (double the recipe for more)

Crisp and chewy, this gluten-free option is the perfect substitute for the Super Simple Pizza Dough (page 20). It'll need to bake twice—once without toppings and again when you've loaded it up—so get your oven ready!

TOOLS TO GATHER

Measuring spoons and cups

Kitchen thermometer

Small mixing bowl

Wooden spoon or rubber spatula

Stand mixer or large mixing bowl with electric beaters

Baking sheet

Timer

HINT

Don't try to make this crust by kneading the dough with your hands. The gluten-free flour won't form a tasty crust that way.

¾ cup warm **water** (between 110°F and 120°F)

1 package (2¼ teaspoons) **active dry yeast**

1 tablespoon **sugar**

2 cups **gluten-free flour blend**

1 teaspoon **salt**

1 large **egg**

3 teaspoons **extra-virgin olive oil**, divided

1 teaspoon **cider vinegar**

1. **Wake up the yeast.** Heat the water either in a microwave-safe measuring cup in the microwave, by running the hot tap water, or using a kettle. Measure the temperature with a kitchen thermometer. Add hot or cold water as needed until the water reaches between 110°F and 120°F. Pour the yeast into a small mixing bowl, then add the sugar and warm water. Stir with the wooden spoon. Let the yeast sit for 5 minutes until the mixture is bubbly and smells like bread.

2. **Combine the ingredients.** In a stand mixer or large bowl, combine the flour and salt. Add the egg, 1 teaspoon of olive oil (save the other 2 teaspoons for the next step), vinegar, and the yeast mixture. Mix on low speed for 1 minute.

3. **Form the crust.** Drizzle the remaining 2 teaspoons of olive oil onto the center of the baking sheet. Scrape the dough from the bowl onto the oil. Rub a little oil onto clean fingers, then use your fingers to press the dough out, starting from the center and working out to the edges until it's round and measures about 12 inches across.

4. **Rest the dough.** Preheat the oven to 450°F. While the oven heats, let the dough rest on the baking sheet for about 15 minutes.

5. **Prebake the crust.** Set the timer for 8 minutes and bake the crust (without any toppings) just until it's set, 8 to 10 minutes. The crust should look smooth but not shiny.

6. **Add your toppings.** Choose from any of the topping ideas in chapters 5 to 8, or make up your own combination, and top your pizza dough!

7. **Finish baking.** Return the pizza to the oven. Set the timer and bake for 8 to 10 minutes, depending on how loaded it is with toppings (the more toppings, the longer the pizza will take to cook).

So what's the difference between a pizza that has gluten and a pizza that's gluten free? Flours are made from starches, typically grains, which contain gluten. But flours can also be made from non-grain starches like almonds or even potatoes. Hence, gluten-free flours!

3
SAUCE CLASS

In this class you'll learn how to make your own pizza sauces—from fresh tomato sauce to super green pesto to the ooiest-gooiest cheese sauce you've ever seen. Most recipes in this book use one of these sauces (and sometimes you'll add more ingredients), but you can also mix and match each sauce with any toppings or crust combinations you like. That's part of the fun of making your own pizza.

Using the Stove

Some sauces, such as white sauces or meat sauces, need to be cooked on the stove-top. These sauces are more advanced—and completely optional—but definitely delicious.

Just make sure to **have an adult present** if you're working with an open flame on the stovetop. Here are a few tips every pizza chef should know:

PAY ATTENTION: Never try to do multiple things at the same time when you're cooking on the stovetop! That's how accidents happen.

USE OVEN MITTS: Use an oven mitt to touch the pan handle, even if you *think* the handle is cool.

KEEP PAN HANDLES TURNED IN: Always direct the handle of the pan away from your body so no one can accidentally bump the handle and either knock the pan off the stove or spill the sauce.

DON'T TOUCH THE BURNER: Burners stay hot for a long time after they've been turned off. Never touch a burner, even after you've finished using it.

KEEP HAIR AND LOOSE CLOTHING TIED BACK: Ponytails, headbands, and aprons keep you clean and safe.

CLEAN UP: When the stove has cooled off, always wipe up any spills so they don't start smoking (or burning) next time you use the burners.

Using a Blender or Food Processor

To get the best and smoothest no-cook pizza sauces, such as tomato or pesto (see the recipes on pages 33 and 36!), you'll want to use a food processor or blender. Here's how you can get great results every time:

1. **ADD CHUNKY INGREDIENTS FIRST:** Garlic, cheese, or nuts should be ground up before adding any wet ingredients.

2. **USE A RUBBER OR SILICONE SPATULA TO SCRAPE THE SIDES:** If you see ingredients getting hung up on the sides of the bowl, stop the blender or food processor (always wait until it has completely stopped before you open the lid) and use a spatula to scrape those bits down into the rest of the mixture.

3. **ALWAYS REMEMBER TO PUT THE TOP ON**: Don't turn on a blender or food processor without first making sure the lid is on tightly or you'll have the biggest mess you've ever seen!

4. **USE THE "PULSE" BUTTON**: Instead of turning a blender or food processor on by using the "On" button, which makes the machine work nonstop, you can push the "Pulse" button, which blends or processes only while you have your finger pressed down on the button and turns off when you let go.

5. **TURN OFF THE MACHINE FOR A TASTE TEST**: When you've stopped the blender or food processor, use a clean spoon to take a tiny taste of your sauce. Does it need more salt? More of another flavor? Add whatever you think it needs, replace the lid, and pulse a couple more times. Then use another clean spoon to test it again.

SUPER EASY RED SAUCE

PREP TIME: 10 minutes

MAKES: about
1½ cups (enough for
2 [13-inch] pizzas)

TOOLS TO GATHER

Measuring cups and spoons

Kid-safe knife

Food processor or blender

Can opener

Strainer

DOUBLE IT

Double the recipe and freeze
half of the sauce for another
pizza night. To freeze extra
sauce, pour it into the cups of
a muffin pan and put the pan
in the freezer overnight. When
the sauce cups are completely
solid, transfer them to a
freezer bag, and you'll have
the perfect amount of sauce
for each pizza next time.

SWAP IT

Add ½ tablespoon of balsamic
vinegar or dried herbs (such
as oregano, rosemary, or onion
powder) for another burst of
flavor.

This simple sauce comes together without any cooking
at all. You can use fresh tomatoes when they're in season,
or rely on canned tomatoes, which are available any time.
Here's a good tip: Remember to squeeze out the extra juices
from the tomatoes and your sauce will be just the right
consistency.

1 **garlic clove**,
 coarsely chopped

¾ cup **diced tomatoes**,
 (about 1 medium tomato or
 half a 14.5-ounce can)

1 tablespoon **extra-virgin
 olive oil**

½ teaspoon **sugar**

5 to 6 fresh **basil** leaves, or
 1 teaspoon dried basil

½ teaspoon **salt**

¼ teaspoon freshly ground
 black pepper

1. **Chop the garlic in the food processor.** In a food processor, pulse the garlic two or three times (hold your finger
   down on the pulse button and count to three each time)
   until it's finely chopped.

2. **Strain the tomatoes.** Open the can of tomatoes and pour
   them into a strainer over the sink. The extra liquid will
   drain away.

3. **Purée the sauce.** Add the tomatoes, olive oil, sugar, basil,
   salt, and pepper to the garlic in the food processor. Turn
   the food processor on and let it run for 20 to 30 seconds,
   until all the ingredients are combined into a smooth
   red sauce.

For Laughs!

How do you fix a broken pizza? *With tomato paste.*

GREEN MACHINE PESTO

PREP TIME: 10 minutes
MAKES: about 2 cups

TOOLS TO GATHER

Measuring cups and spoons
Grater
Food processor
Rubber or silicone spatula

SWAP IT

Make a dairy-free version by using ½ cup of pine nuts and skipping the cheese altogether. For nut-free pesto, boost the cheese to ¾ cup and add the juice and zest of 1 lemon. Don't have any pine nuts? Walnuts or almonds will work fine.

Classic fresh pesto has the perfect combination of salt, fat, and fresh flavor to dazzle your taste buds. If you want even more of a nutritional boost, substitute half the basil for baby spinach.

3 **garlic** cloves

⅓ cup **pine nuts**

2 cups fresh **basil** leaves

½ cup freshly grated **Parmesan cheese** (about 2 ounces)

½ cup **extra-virgin olive oil**

¼ teaspoon **salt**, plus more to taste

2 or 3 grinds of **black pepper**

1. **Pulse the garlic and pine nuts.** Pulse the garlic cloves and pine nuts in the food processor (hold your finger down on the pulse button and count to 3 each time) until the mixture is chopped.

2. **Add the basil and cheese.** Open the food processor lid to add the basil leaves and cheese. Pulse 2 or 3 more times until the mixture looks chunky and green.

3. **Pour in the olive oil.** Replace the lid of the food processor but leave the top hole open. Turn the food processor on low speed and slowly add the olive oil. When all the oil is in, stop the food processor and scrape down the sides of the bowl with a spatula to get any ingredients stuck on the sides down into the mixture. Pulse again.

4. **Add salt and pepper.** Add the salt and pepper, then use a clean spoon to taste the pesto. Add more salt or pepper if you think the pesto needs it.

Did You Know?

Pesto originally comes from Liguria, Italy, but the French have their own version, too: It's from Provence, has no nuts or cheese, and is called *pistou*.

EXTRA CHEESY WHITE SAUCE

PREP TIME: 5 minutes
COOK TIME: 15 minutes
MAKES: about 2 cups

TOOLS TO GATHER

Measuring cups and spoons
Grater
Small saucepan
Wooden spoon or rubber spatula
Whisk

Although pizza may be Italian, the process of cooking a thick, white sauce is actually French: It's called making a *roux*. By combining melted butter with flour then adding liquid and cheese, you'll get a rich and creamy sauce that's perfect for many pizzas.

2 tablespoons **butter**

1 tablespoon **extra-virgin olive oil**

3 tablespoons **all-purpose flour**

1 cup **milk**

½ cup freshly grated **Parmesan cheese**

1 teaspoon **Italian seasoning** blend (or any mix of dried oregano and basil)

1 teaspoon **garlic powder**

¼ teaspoon **salt**

2 or 3 grinds of **black pepper**

1. **Melt the butter and oil.** In a small saucepan over medium-low heat, melt the butter and oil together.

2. **Cook the flour.** Add the flour to the pan. It'll look like a clumpy paste. With a wooden spoon, carefully stir the flour around in the butter until the flour starts to turn brown. This might take about 2 minutes.

3. **Add the remaining ingredients.** With a whisk in one hand and the milk in your other, slowly pour the milk into the pan, whisking all the time. Move quickly to add the cheese, Italian seasonings, garlic powder, salt, and pepper, then stir the sauce again. Keep stirring the sauce until all the cheese has melted and the ingredients are combined, about 5 minutes. Remove the pan from the heat. The sauce is done!

Did You Know?

Real Parmesan cheese is always one of two kinds—Parmigiano-Reggiano or Grana Padano—and both are from specific regions of Italy.

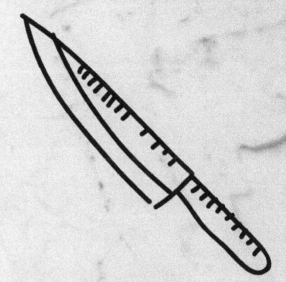

4
TOPPINGS CLASS

Whether it's pepperoni, mushrooms, black olives, or extra cheese, nothing makes a pizza more personal than the toppings you choose. And when you make your own pizza, you get to call all the shots. But it isn't simply a matter of throwing ingredients on top of your pizza; it helps to know certain skills, such as the different ways you can use a knife to make the best shapes for your toppings, or learning which ingredients work best together. And that's what you're going to learn in this chapter.

Learning to Cut

Hold the handle of the knife as though you're shaking hands with the handle. The blade should be facing away from you, with the sharp edge down toward the cutting board. The closer to the blade you hold the handle, the more control you'll have when cutting, but be careful: Don't touch the sharp edge of the blade!

USE BOTH HANDS. One hand should hold the knife by the handle while the other hand steadies the food. The safe way to hold food while you're cutting is to curl your fingers under so your hand makes a "C" shape, and keep your hand as far away from the blade as possible.

ALWAYS ROCK THE BLADE. Slice down and away from yourself, moving the knife like a boat on the sea.

Hint!

- An extra-large cutting board is easier to use than a small board. You won't have to worry about ingredients falling off the sides of the board, and there will be plenty of working space.

- Cutting an onion or tomato? Ask an adult to slice a tiny sliver off one side of the food item to make a flat edge. Lay the flat edge on the cutting board so the food doesn't wobble. You'll be able to slice it more easily if it isn't rolling around.

How to Slice a Tomato or Bell Pepper

Use these instructions when slicing tomatoes or bell peppers! Start with a large cutting board and a small, sharp knife.

1. **LOCATE THE STEM AND REMOVE THE CORE.** Poke the tip of the knife into the tomato near the stem and cut in a circle until you can pop out the center.

2. **CUT THE TOMATO IN HALF.** Use your knife to cut down the center of the tomato.

3. **FLIP.** Place both halves on the cutting board, with the cut sides down.

4. **SLICE.** Slice the tomato, working on one half at a time.

How to Chop Herbs

Fresh herbs like basil, oregano, and parsley add a powerful punch of flavor to pizza. The trick to getting the most flavor is chopping them without damaging the herbs—or your fingers.

OPTION 1: The classic method for chopping fresh herbs is to roll the herbs into a bundle. Place the bundle on a cutting board, hold it with one hand (remembering to tuck your fingers under in a "C" shape and keep them away from the blade), and carefully slice your way down the bundle from the tip toward your holding hand.

OPTION 2: Try this simple trick for chopped fresh herbs fast: Place the herbs in a tall glass. Use kitchen shears (scissors) to snip them into pieces.

How to Dice an Onion

Whether it's in the sauce or a topping, nothing adds bite to pizza like onion. Here's the trick to cutting an onion into equally sized pieces:

1. **SLICE THE ONION IN HALF.** Using a cutting board and large knife, slice the onion in half, cutting through the root end (ask an adult if you're not sure which end this is). Remove the outer layer of skin from the onion.

2. **PLACE THE CUT SIDE DOWN.** Working with one half of the onion at a time, point the tip of the knife into the onion near the root; push down and cut five or six vertical slices, but don't cut through the root.

3. **ROTATE THE ONION.** Turn the onion half so the flat side is facing away from you. Slice your knife horizontally, moving toward your holding hand (and the root). Stop before you get to the root and repeat, working your way up the onion from nearest the cutting board to the top.

4. **SLICE AGAIN.** Holding the onion by the root, now start slicing straight down. Start with the edge farthest away from your hand. Every time your knife slices down across the onion, you're creating tiny squares of diced onion.

Taste the Seasons

Every season, nature produces new foods for us to enjoy. Sure, most grocery stores carry foods such as fresh tomatoes all year long, but that's only because some foods are grown in greenhouses in warm areas, then hauled to stores across the country. Eating food in season has many benefits! It preserves the environment, offers support to local farmers, and gives you the best tasting, most nutritious food of all.

What's in season for your pizza?

 SPRING: mushrooms, spring onions, pineapples, spinach

 SUMMER: bell peppers, raspberries, strawberries, tomatoes, zucchini

 FALL: kiwi fruit, spinach, sweet potatoes

 WINTER: beets, kale, potatoes

 ALL YEAR: garlic, onions

5

OLD SCHOOL CLASSICS

Your favorite food is only minutes away! Get ready to dig in to a good ol' plain cheese pizza, a flavorful pepperoni pie, or a luscious ricotta-spinach filling riding atop a deep dish crust—because you'll want to make these traditional pizzas over and over again.

CHEESE PIZZA

PREP TIME: 20 minutes
COOK TIME: 20 minutes
MAKES: 2 (13-inch) pizzas

TOOLS TO GATHER

Measuring spoons and cups

Grater

2 pizza pans, pizza stones, or baking sheets

Paper towel (optional)

Cutting board or clean counter space

Kid-safe knife

Rolling pin (optional)

Large spoon

Timer

SWAP IT

Use Green Machine Pesto (page 36) in place of Super Easy Red Sauce.

Have you ever met a kid who didn't like cheese pizza? Me neither! You can whip up an ooey-gooey cheese pizza of your own in the same amount of time it takes to call for delivery.

2 tablespoons **extra-virgin olive oil**

1 batch **Super Simple Pizza Dough** (page 20)

1 tablespoon **cornmeal**, for dusting

1 batch (1½ cups) **Super Easy Red Sauce** (page 33)

2 cups shredded **mozzarella cheese**

1. **Preheat the oven and prep the pans.** Adjust the oven racks to the lowest positions. Turn the oven on to 400°F. While the oven warms up, drizzle the olive oil into the pizza pans and use clean fingers (or a paper towel) to spread the oil evenly.

2. **Arrange the pizza dough.** If you haven't already cut the Super Simple Pizza Dough in half (see page 20), do it now using a kid-safe knife. Now you need to stretch each piece of dough into 2 circles, each about the size of your pans. Dust the work surface with the cornmeal. Using either your hands or a rolling pin, stretch or roll the dough in one direction, then rotate the dough and repeat, making sure you rotate the dough after each stretch or roll so it stays as round as possible. Place 1 pizza dough circle in each greased pan.

3. **Add the sauce.** Use a large spoon to ladle about ¾ cup of the red sauce on to each piece of dough. Use the back of the spoon to spread the sauce evenly.

4. **Top with the cheese.** Sprinkle each pizza with 1 cup each of shredded mozzarella cheese.

5. **Bake.** [STOP] Ask an adult to help put the pans in the oven. Set the timer for 14 minutes and bake until the pizza crusts look golden brown and the cheese is melted and bubbly, 14 to 20 minutes.

6. **Slice.** Allow the pizzas to cool for 2 to 3 minutes before slicing, and be careful when you take the first bite. Fresh pizza is delicious—but also very hot!

For Laughs!
Want to hear a joke about pizza? *Never mind. It's too cheesy.*

PEPPERONI PIZZA

PREP TIME: 20 minutes
COOK TIME: 20 minutes
MAKES: 2 (13-inch) pizzas

TOOLS TO GATHER

Measuring spoons and cups

Grater

2 pizza pans, pizza stones, or baking sheets

Paper towel (optional)

Kid-safe knife

Cutting board or clean counter space

Rolling pin (optional)

Large spoon

Timer

MAKE IT YOUR OWN

Pepperoni pizza is a classic. These days you can get pepperoni that's miniature-sized, made from turkey, and even vegetarian. Have fun with it!

For Laughs!

What pizza do dogs love?
Pupperoni!

What's the most popular pizza topping in the United States? That's right—it's pepperoni!.

2 tablespoons **extra-virgin olive oil**

1 batch **Super Simple Pizza Dough** (page 20)

1 tablespoon **cornmeal**, for dusting

1 batch (1½ cups) **Super Easy Red Sauce** (page 33)

1½ cups shredded **mozzarella cheese**

1 cup sliced **pepperoni**

1. **Preheat the oven and prep the pan(s).** Adjust the oven racks to the lowest positions. Turn the oven on to 400°F. Drizzle the olive oil into the pans and use clean fingers (or a paper towel) to spread the oil evenly.

2. **Arrange the pizza dough.** If you haven't already cut the Super Simple Pizza Dough in half (see page 20), do it now using a kid-safe knife. Now you need to stretch each piece of dough into 2 circles, each about the size of your pans. Dust the work surface with the cornmeal. Using either your hands or a rolling pin, stretch or roll the dough in one direction, then rotate the dough and repeat, making sure you rotate the dough after each stretch or roll so it stays as round as possible. Place 1 pizza dough circle in each greased pan.

3. **Add the sauce.** Use a large spoon to ladle about ¾ cup of the red sauce on each pizza. Use the back of the spoon to spread the sauce evenly.

4. **Top with the cheese and pepperoni.** Sprinkle each pizza with ¾ cup of shredded mozzarella cheese. Place slices of pepperoni all over each pizza.

5. **Bake.** 🛑 Ask an adult to help put the pans in the oven. Set the timer for 14 minutes and bake until the crusts look golden brown and the cheese is melted and bubbly, 14 to 20 minutes.

6. **Slice.** Allow the pizzas to cool for 2 to 3 minutes before slicing, and be careful when you take the first bite. Fresh pizza is delicious—but also very hot!

MARGHERITA PIZZA

PREP TIME: 20 minutes
COOK TIME: 20 minutes
MAKES: 2 (13-inch) pizzas

TOOLS TO GATHER

Measuring spoons and cups

2 pizza pans, pizza stones, or baking sheets

Paper towel (optional)

Cutting board or clean counter space

Kid-safe knife

Rolling pin (optional)

Large spoon

Timer

SWAP IT

A gluten-free crust (page 26) would work beautifully with this pizza.

Did you know this pizza is named after a queen? Margherita was the queen of Italy when a pizza maker from Naples created this dish just for her in the official colors of Italy's flag: red, white, and green. Bonus: It's the most delicious pizza I've ever had, so trust me when I say it's worth a try!

2 tablespoons **extra-virgin olive oil**

1 batch **Super Simple Pizza Dough** (page 20)

1 tablespoon **cornmeal**, for dusting

1 batch (1½ cups) **Super Easy Red Sauce** (page 33)

16 ounces fresh **mozzarella cheese**

4 or 5 fresh **basil** leaves

1. **Preheat the oven and prep the pans.** Adjust the oven racks to the lowest positions. Turn the oven on to 400°F. While it warms up, drizzle the olive oil in the pans and use clean fingers (or a paper towel) to spread the oil evenly.

2. **Arrange the pizza dough.** If you haven't already cut the Super Simple Pizza Dough in half (see page 20), do it now using a kid-safe knife. Now you need to stretch each piece of dough into 2 circles, each about the size of your pans. Dust the work surface with the cornmeal. Using either your hands or a rolling pin, stretch or roll the dough in one direction, then rotate the dough and repeat, making sure you rotate the dough after each stretch or roll so it stays as round as possible. Place 1 pizza dough circle in each greased pan.

3. **Add the sauce.** Use a large spoon to ladle about ¾ cup of the red sauce on each pizza. Use the back of the spoon to spread the sauce evenly.

4. **Top with the cheese.** Use a kid-safe knife to cut through the fresh mozzarella cheese and arrange the slices on the pizzas.

5. **Bake.** 🛑 Ask an adult to help put the pizzas in the oven. Set the timer for 14 minutes and bake until the crusts look golden brown and the cheese is melted and bubbly, 14 to 20 minutes.

6. **Top with the basil.** Place the basil on top of the hot cheese just after it comes out of the oven. Watch out! The cheese will be really hot. You can ask an adult to help, if you want.

7. **Slice.** Wait at least 2 to 3 minutes before transferring the pizzas to a cutting board to slice. Margherita pizza is especially gooey, and that cheese will be very hot!

For Laughs!

How does a pizza introduce itself? *Slice to meet you!*

SAUSAGE, PEPPERS & PESTO PIZZA

PREP TIME: 30 minutes
COOK TIME: 15 minutes
MAKES: 2 (13-inch) pizzas

TOOLS TO GATHER

Measuring spoons and cups

Grater

Cutting board or clean counter space

Kid-safe knife

Skillet

Wooden spoon or silicone spatula

2 pizza pans, pizza stones, or baking sheets

Paper towel (optional)

Rolling pin (optional)

Large spoon

Timer

MAKE IT YOUR OWN

Use ground beef (or turkey) instead of sausage + swap the mozzarella cheese for Cheddar = cheeseburger pizza!

This thick and hearty pizza packs a serious flavor punch!

1 **bell pepper**

16 ounces **ground sausage** (turkey, pork, or chicken)

2 tablespoons **extra-virgin olive oil**

1 batch **Super Simple Pizza Dough** (page 20)

1 tablespoon **cornmeal** for dusting

1 batch (1½ cups) **Green Machine Pesto** (page 36)

1½ cups shredded **mozzarella cheese**

1. **Cook the peppers and sausage.** Use a kid-safe knife to cut the bell pepper into strips. Put a skillet over medium-high heat on the stovetop and cook the sausage and peppers, breaking up the sausage with a wooden spoon, until the sausage is browned and the pepper strips get soft on their edges.

2. **Preheat the oven and prep the pans.** Adjust the oven racks to the lowest positions. Turn the oven on to 400°F. While the oven warms up, drizzle the olive oil into the pans and use clean fingers (or a paper towel) to spread the oil evenly.

3. **Arrange the pizza dough.** If you haven't already cut the Super Simple Pizza Dough in half (see page 20), do it now using a kid-safe knife. Now you need to stretch each piece of dough into 2 circles, each about the size of your pans. Dust the work surface with the cornmeal. Using either your hands or a rolling pin, stretch or roll the dough in one direction, then rotate the dough and repeat, making sure you rotate the dough after each stretch or roll so it stays as round as possible. Place 1 pizza dough circle in each greased pan.

4. **Add the sauce.** Use a large spoon to ladle about ¾ cup of pesto on to each pizza. Use the back of the spoon to spread the pesto evenly.

5. **Top with the sausage and peppers.** Add half the sausage and pepper mixture to each pizza.

6. **Add the cheese.** Sprinkle each pizza with ¾ cup of shredded mozzarella cheese.

7. **Bake.** STOP Ask an adult to help put the pizzas in the oven. Set the timer for 12 minutes and bake until the crusts look golden brown and the cheese is melted and bubbly, 12 to 15 minutes.

8. **Slice.** Wait at least 2 to 3 minutes before transferring the pizzas to a cutting board to slice.

Did You Know?

The word "pizza" comes from the Latin word *picea*, which means "the blackening of the crust by fire."

RICOTTA & SPINACH DEEP DISH PIZZA

PREP TIME: 45 minutes
COOK TIME: 29 minutes
MAKES: 1 (13-inch) pizza

TOOLS TO GATHER

Measuring spoons and cups

Grater

Cast iron skillet or 2-inch-deep pizza pan

Cutting board or clean counter space

Rolling pin

Small mixing bowl

Kid-safe knife

Wooden spoon

Long metal spatula

Serrated knife (ask an adult to use this)

Large spoon

Timer

DOUBLE IT

Want to make more than one pizza? Use a full batch of Cornmeal Pizza Dough (see page 24) and double the rest of the ingredients.

Get ready for green pizza! This rich and colorful pie makes a hearty vegetarian meal, sure to satisfy anyone craving a majorly thick crust. If you don't have frozen spinach, not to worry—just microwave 3 cups of fresh spinach with 2 tablespoons of water for 2 minutes, and then drain.

Butter, at room temperature, for greasing

Cornmeal, for dusting

½ batch **Cornmeal Pizza Dough** (page 24)

3 cups shredded **mozzarella cheese**, divided

1½ cups frozen **spinach**, thawed and drained (or see the headnote if you are using fresh), divided

1 teaspoon finely chopped **garlic**

9 ounces **provolone cheese**, thinly sliced (about 12 slices)

2 cups **Super Easy Red Sauce** (page 33)

½ cup **ricotta cheese**

3 tablespoons freshly grated **pecorino Romano**

Dried **oregano**, for topping

1. **Heat the oven.** Adjust the oven racks to the top and bottom positions. Turn the oven on to 500°F.

2. **Prepare the pan.** Butter the bottom and sides of a cast iron skillet or a 2-inch-deep round pizza pan.

3. **Prepare the dough.** Dust the work surface with a generous amount of cornmeal. Place the dough on the surface, then coat both sides with cornmeal. Flatten the dough a bit, then roll it out into a 17-inch circle (it should be larger than your skillet or pizza pan). Lift the dough and carefully lower it onto the skillet. Lift the edges of the dough so that they sink into the corners of the skillet. Press all along the inside edge to make sure the dough is firmly tucked against the pan.

4. **Assemble the pizza.** Sprinkle 2½ cups of the mozzarella cheese on top of the dough in an even layer. Add 1 cup of spinach over the mozzarella (put the remaining ½ cup of spinach in a small mixing bowl for use in step 7). Sprinkle with the garlic and top with the provolone slices.

5. **Trim the dough.** If there's any dough still hanging over the edges of the skillet, run the rolling pin over the rim to cut it off.

6. **Bake.** **STOP** Ask an adult to help put the skillet in the oven (it's heavy!), on the bottom rack. Set the timer for 15 minutes. When the timer sounds, **STOP** ask an adult to help rotate the skillet (turn it around). Set the timer for another 12 minutes and bake the pizza until the cheese is melted and the crust is a rich golden brown.

7. **Prepare the sauce and cheese topping.** While the pizza is baking, prepare the Super Easy Red Sauce. Then, with a wooden spoon, stir the ricotta cheese into the spinach in the small bowl.

8. **Add more cheese.** **STOP** Ask an adult to take the skillet out of the oven, then spoon the tomato sauce and the spinach and ricotta mixture on top. Finish by sprinkling the remaining shredded mozzarella over the spinach and ricotta. **STOP** Ask an adult to put the skillet back in the oven, on the top rack, for 2 minutes to melt the shredded cheese.

9. **Loosen the dough.** **STOP** Ask an adult to remove the skillet from the oven. Run a long metal spatula around the inside of the skillet to loosen the pizza from the pan. Then, use the spatula to lift an edge and check the bottom of the crust. It should be browned and crisp. If it needs more time, **STOP** ask an adult to return the skillet to the bottom oven rack for 1 minute.

10. **Finish and serve.** Using the spatula, and being careful not to pierce the bottom of the crust, lift the pizza from the skillet and transfer it to a cutting board. Finish with a sprinkle of pecorino and oregano for extra flavor. **STOP** Ask an adult to use a serrated knife to cut the pizza into 6 large wedges.

For Laughs!

Why are spinach leaves never lonely? *Because they come in bunches!*

6

NEW SCHOOL FAVORITES

If you love the combination of sweet and tangy flavors, this is the chapter for you! There's ham and pineapple, barbecued chicken smothered in two kinds of smoky cheese, apples with cheddar, and more. These pizzas are a great addition to your classics recipe collection.

BARBECUE CHICKEN PIZZA

PREP TIME: 35 minutes
COOK TIME: 35 minutes
MAKES: 2 (13-inch) pizzas

TOOLS TO GATHER

Measuring cups and spoons

Grater

Kid-safe knife

Pastry brush

Parchment paper

Rolling pin

Small mixing bowl

Small baking dish

2 pizza pans, 2 pizza stones, or baking sheets

Timer

SWAP IT

For a less spicy sauce, substitute ketchup for half the barbecue sauce.
Or substitute barbecued brisket or ribs for the chicken for a more Southern kick!

Loaded with zesty (but not too spicy!) sauce, this crispy chicken pizza is the perfect summer meal.

1 batch **Super Simple Pizza Dough** (page 20)

2 teaspoons **extra-virgin olive oil**, plus more for brushing

1 cup **barbecue sauce**, divided, plus 2 tablespoons

2 (8-ounce) boneless, skinless **chicken breasts** (or precooked rotisserie chicken: skip step 4)

1 teaspoon **salt**

½ teaspoon freshly ground **black pepper**

1 cup (about 4 ounces) shredded **smoked Gouda cheese**

1 cup (about 4 ounces) shredded **mozzarella cheese**

1 small **red onion**, thinly sliced (optional)

1. **Heat the oven.** Adjust the racks to the lowest positions. Turn the oven on to 450°F.

2. **Prepare the dough.** If you haven't already cut the Super Simple Pizza Dough in half (see page 20), do it now using a kid-safe knife. Brush a piece of parchment paper with a little olive oil. Place 1 piece of dough on top of the parchment paper and use a rolling pin to flatten it out into a 13-inch circle. Cover the dough with a second piece of parchment paper and set it aside. (Repeat with the second piece of dough.)

3. **Prep the sauce.** In a small bowl, mix ¼ cup of barbecue sauce with 2 teaspoons of olive oil.

4. **Cook the chicken.** Set the chicken breasts in a small baking dish, sprinkle with the salt and pepper, then brush with the barbecue sauce. Roast for 20 minutes until the chicken is cooked through. Remove the dish from the oven and allow the chicken to cool. Use a kid-safe knife to cut the chicken into small cubes.

5. **Top the pizza.** Remove the top piece of parchment paper from 1 dough circle. Spread ⅓ cup of barbecue sauce evenly on each pizza dough, leaving a border around the edge without sauce (about an inch). Top with the cut-up chicken, Gouda, mozzarella, and red onion (if using). Pick up the edges of the parchment paper and move the pizza to a pizza pan. (Repeat with the second dough circle.)

6. **Bake.** STOP Ask an adult to help put the pizzas in the oven. Set the timer for 12 minutes and bake until the crusts look golden brown and the cheese is melted and bubbly, 12 to 15 minutes.

7. **Slice.** Allow the pizzas to cool for 2 to 3 minutes before slicing, and be careful when you take the first bite. Fresh pizza is delicious—but also very hot!

Did You Know?
Barbecue cooking means to cook very slowly at a lower temperature than grilling.

HAM & PINEAPPLE PIZZA

PREP TIME: 20 minutes
COOK TIME: 15 minutes
MAKES: 1 (13-inch pizza)

TOOLS TO GATHER

Measuring spoons and cups

Grater

Pastry brush

Parchment paper

Rolling pin

Pizza pan, pizza stone, or baking sheet

Timer

MAKE IT YOUR OWN

Add fresh green peppers for an extra flavorful crunch!

DOUBLE IT

This recipe only makes one pizza, so if you think that's not going to be enough, just double up the ingredients to make two!

As a kid growing up on the West Coast, this was the *only* kind of pizza we ever had. And it's still my favorite today: sweet and salty all at once.

Extra-virgin olive oil, for brushing

½ batch **Super Simple Pizza Dough** (page 20)

½ batch (¾ cup) **Super Easy Red Sauce** (page 33)

3 cups shredded **mozzarella cheese**

1 cup sliced or chopped cooked **ham** or **Canadian bacon**

1 cup **pineapple** chunks (canned or fresh)

3 slices **bacon**, cooked and crumbled (optional)

1. **Heat the oven.** Adjust the oven rack to the lowest position. Turn the oven on to 475°F.

2. **Prepare the dough.** Brush a piece of parchment paper with a little olive oil. Place the dough on top of the parchment paper and use a rolling pin to flatten it out into a 13-inch circle.

3. **Top the pizza.** Brush the dough with a thin layer of olive oil. Spread the red sauce on the dough, leaving a 1-inch border clear of sauce. Sprinkle with the cheese, ham, pineapple, and bacon (if using).

4. **Bake.** 🛑 Ask an adult to help put the pizza in the oven. Set the timer for 12 minutes and bake until the crust looks golden brown and the cheese is melted and bubbly, 12 to 15 minutes.

5. **Slice.** Allow the pizza to cool for 2 to 3 minutes before slicing, and be careful when you take the first bite. Fresh pizza is delicious—but also very hot!

For Laughs!

When is an apple not an apple? *When it's a pineapple!*

SAVORY APPLE WITH WHITE CHEDDAR PIZZA

PREP TIME: 30 minutes
COOK TIME: 35 minutes
MAKES: 2 (13-inch) pizzas

TOOLS TO GATHER

Measuring spoons and cups

Grater

Kid-safe knife

Pastry brush

Parchment paper

Rolling pin

Large skillet

Wooden spoon or silicone spatula

2 pizza pans, 2 pizza stones, or baking sheets

Timer

MAKE IT YOUR OWN

Try Gruyère instead of Cheddar for a creamier result.

You may be thinking: apples on pizza? But trust me, sweet and juicy apples go perfectly with the creamy tartness of Cheddar cheese. This is a grown-up flavor combination!

1 batch **Super Simple Pizza Dough** (page 20)

1 tablespoon **extra-virgin olive oil**, plus more for brushing

1 tablespoon **butter**

2 **yellow onions**, cut into thin rings

2 teaspoons **Dijon mustard**

1 batch (2 cups) **Extra Cheesy White Sauce** (page 37)

3 or 4 **baking apples** (such as Granny Smith), cored, peeled, and thinly sliced

1 cup shredded sharp **Cheddar cheese**

1 tablespoon finely chopped fresh **thyme** leaves, plus more for topping (optional)

1 teaspoon **salt**

½ teaspoon freshly ground **black pepper**

1. **Heat the oven.** Position the racks in the top of the oven. Turn the oven on to 400°F.

2. **Prepare the dough.** If you haven't already cut the Super Simple Pizza Dough in half (see page 20), do it now using a kid-safe knife. Brush a piece of parchment paper with a little olive oil. Place 1 piece of dough on top of the parchment paper and use a rolling pin to flatten it out into a 13-inch circle. Cover the dough with another piece of parchment paper and set it aside. Repeat with the second piece of dough.

3. **Cook the onions.** In a large skillet over medium heat, melt the butter and oil. Add the onions and cook, stirring occasionally, until lightly browned, about 15 minutes.

4. **Prepare the sauce.** Add the mustard to the cheese sauce and stir.

5. **Top the pizza.** Remove the top piece of parchment paper from 1 dough circle. Brush the dough circle with a thin layer of olive oil. On the dough circle, spread half the white sauce then arrange half the apples and half the cooked onions on top. Sprinkle with half the Cheddar cheese, the thyme, and half the salt and pepper. Repeat for the second pizza. Pick up the edges of the parchment paper and move 1 pizza to a pizza pan. Repeat with the second pizza.

6. **Bake.** STOP Ask an adult to help put the pizzas in the oven. Set the timer for 20 minutes and bake until the crust is golden and the cheese is melted and bubbly.

7. **Slice.** Allow the pizzas to cool for 2 to 3 minutes before slicing, and be careful when you take the first bite. Fresh pizza is delicious—but also very hot!

Did You Know?

Granny Smith apples get their name from the Australian woman who first developed the trees with that signature tart, green fruit: Her name was Maria Anne Smith.

PESTO CHICKEN DEEP DISH PIZZA

PREP TIME: 30 minutes
COOK TIME: 47 minutes
MAKES: 1 (13-inch pizza)

TOOLS TO GATHER

Measuring spoons and cups

Grater

Cast iron skillet or 2-inch-deep pizza pan

Cutting board or clean counter space

Rolling pin

Small baking dish

Timer

Kid-safe knife

Long metal spatula

Serrated knife

MAKE IT YOUR OWN

Substitute half the Green Machine Pesto for Super Easy Red Sauce (see page 33) and mix it together for a zesty alternative.

DOUBLE IT

Want to make more than one pizza? Use a full batch of Cornmeal Pizza Dough and double the rest of the ingredients.

I hope you're hungry! One slice of this super thick and hearty pizza—along with a crispy salad or handful of raw veggies—will fill the tummy of even the hungriest pizza baker.

Butter, at room temperature, for greasing

Cornmeal, for dusting

½ batch **Cornmeal Pizza Dough** (page 24)

2 (8-ounce) boneless, skinless **chicken breasts** (or precooked rotisserie chicken: skip step 4)

1 tablespoon **extra-virgin olive oil**

Salt

Freshly ground **black pepper**

½ batch (1 cup) **Green Machine Pesto** (page 36)

1 cup shredded **mozzarella cheese**

1. **Heat the oven.** Adjust the oven racks to the middle and bottom positions. Turn the oven on to 450°F.

2. **Prepare the pan.** Butter the bottom and sides of a skillet or a 2-inch-deep pizza pan.

3. **Prepare the dough.** Dust the work surface with a generous amount of cornmeal. Place the dough on the surface, then coat both sides with cornmeal. Flatten the dough a bit, then roll it out into a 17-inch circle (it should be larger than your skillet or pizza pan). Lift the dough and carefully lower it onto the skillet. Lift the edges of the dough so that they sink into the corners of the skillet. Press all along the inside edge to make sure the dough is firmly tucked against the pan.

4. **Cook the chicken.** Place the chicken breast in a small baking dish and drizzle with the olive oil. Sprinkle with salt and pepper. **STOP** Ask an adult to help put the dish in the oven. Set the timer for 20 minutes and roast the chicken. Remove the chicken from the oven and let it cool for 3 to 5 minutes, then use a kid-safe knife to cut the chicken into small squares.

5. **Assemble the pizza.** Spread the pesto on the dough. Top with the chicken and mozzarella cheese. Finish with a pinch of salt and pepper.

6. **Bake.** **STOP** Ask an adult to help put the pizza in the oven, on the middle rack. Set the timer for 15 minutes. **STOP** Ask an adult to help you rotate the skillet (turn it around) and then bake the pizza for 12 minutes longer. When the cheese has melted and the crust looks golden, use a spatula to free the side of the crust from the skillet. Peek to check the bottom of the crust. Does it look golden too? If not, **STOP** ask an adult to move the skillet to the bottom rack in the oven. Bake the pizza for 2 minutes longer. **STOP** Ask an adult to help remove the skillet from the oven. Let the pizza cool for a couple of minutes, then **STOP** ask an adult to help you transfer the pizza to a cutting board and to slice it using a serrated knife.

Did You Know?

Basil originates from India, where it's been used as a spice (and medicine!) for more than 5,000 years.

BALSAMIC MUSHROOM & GOAT CHEESE PIZZA

PREP TIME: 30 minutes
COOK TIME: 22 minutes
MAKES: 1 (13-inch) pizza

Full of smoky flavors and with a bit of zing from the sweet
vinegar, this pizza is perfect for kids who love sweet and
savory combinations!

4 tablespoons **extra-virgin
olive oil**, divided, plus more
for brushing

½ batch **Super Simple Pizza
Dough** (page 20)

1 tablespoon **butter**

1 cup **mushrooms**, sliced

Salt, divided

Freshly ground **black
pepper,** divided

2 **garlic** cloves, minced

3 tablespoons
balsamic vinegar

4 ounces sliced **provolone
cheese** (about 6 slices)

4 ounces **goat cheese**,
crumbled

1 tablespoon chopped
fresh **thyme**

1. **Heat the oven.** Adjust the oven rack to the lowest position. Turn the oven on to 450°F.

2. **Prepare the dough.** Brush a piece of parchment paper
   with a little olive oil. Place the dough on top of the
   parchment paper and use a rolling pin to flatten it out
   into a 13-inch circle. Cover the dough with another piece
   of parchment paper and set it aside.

3. **Prepare the mushrooms.** In a skillet over medium heat,
   warm 2 tablespoons of olive oil plus the butter. Add the
   mushrooms and sprinkle with salt and pepper. Cook
   until soft, about 5 minutes. Add the garlic and cook, stirring, for just 30 seconds (or the garlic will burn!). Add the
   balsamic vinegar and cook for 1 more minute. Stir with
   a wooden spoon until the sauce completely coats every
   mushroom.

4. **Top the pizza.** Remove the top piece of parchment paper from the dough. Brush the dough with a thin layer of olive oil. Spread the mushroom mixture on top. Layer the provolone slices over the mushrooms. Top with goat cheese and thyme. Add one more pinch of salt and pepper.

5. **Bake.** STOP Ask an adult to help put the pizza in the oven. Set the timer for 12 minutes, and bake until the crust is golden and the cheese is melted and bubbly, 12 to 15 minutes.

6. **Slice.** Allow the pizzas to cool for 2 to 3 minutes before slicing, and be careful when you take the first bite. Fresh pizza is delicious—but also very hot!

For Laughs!

What room has no walls? *A mushroom!*

7
FLAVORS OF THE WORLD

In this chapter you'll find flavors from Asia, the Mediterranean, and South of the Border on top of a pizza.

THAI CHICKEN PIZZA

PREP TIME: 30 minutes
COOK TIME: 27 minutes
MAKES: 2 (13-inch) pizzas

TOOLS TO GATHER

Measuring spoons and cups

Grater

Kid-safe knife

Pastry brush

Parchment paper

Rolling pin

Small saucepan

Wooden spoon

2 pizza pans, **2** pizza stones, or baking sheets

Timer

MAKE IT YOUR OWN

Use tofu instead of chicken for a vegetarian option.

SWAP IT

Use a store-bought sauce (I like Trader Joe's Satay Peanut Sauce) and skip step **4**. Or, use a store-bought rotisserie chicken and skip step **3**.

What's better than eating one cuisine you like? Eating two! You'll love what happens when Asian cuisine meets Italian. This pizza is sweet and tangy and topped with crunchy peanuts.

For the dough

Extra-virgin olive oil, for brushing

1 batch **Super Simple Pizza Dough** (page 20)

For the chicken

2 tablespoons **extra-virgin olive oil**, divided

2 (8-ounce) boneless, skinless **chicken breasts**

For the peanut sauce

¾ cup **peanut butter**

¼ cup **hoisin sauce**

1 tablespoon **honey**

2 teaspoons **rice wine vinegar**

½ teaspoon **ground ginger**

2 tablespoons **sesame oil**

2 tablespoons **water**

Toppings per pizza

2 cups shredded **mozzarella cheese**, divided

2 **scallions**, thinly sliced diagonally (optional)

½ cup matchstick **carrots**

¼ **bean sprouts**

1 tablespoon chopped **roasted peanuts**

1 tablespoon chopped fresh **cilantro**

1. **Heat the oven.** Adjust the oven racks to the lowest positions. Turn the oven on to 500°F.

2. **Prepare the dough.** If you haven't already cut the Super Simple Pizza Dough in half (see page 20), do it now using a kid-safe knife. Brush a piece of parchment paper with olive oil. Place 1 piece of dough on top of the parchment paper and use a rolling pin to flatten it out into a 13-inch circle. Cover the dough with another piece of parchment paper and set it aside. Repeat this step for the second pizza.

3. **Make the chicken.** Drizzle about 1 teaspoon of olive oil on a baking sheet and place each piece of chicken on top. Pour the rest of the olive oil on the chicken. Roast in the oven for 15 minutes. Allow to cool for about 5 minutes.

4. **Make the peanut sauce.** While the chicken cooks, in a small saucepan over medium-high heat, use a wooden spoon to stir the peanut butter, hoisin sauce, honey, vinegar, ginger, sesame oil, and water. Bring to a boil and cook for 1 minute. Turn the burner off.

5. **Combine the chicken and sauce.** Move the cooked chicken breasts to a cutting board and use a kid-safe knife to cut into bite-size pieces (about 1-inch), about as big as a Lego brick. (Rinse off the baking pan to re-use for the pizza.) Add the chicken to the pan with the peanut sauce and stir to evenly coat the chicken.

6. **Assemble the pizza.** Remove the top piece of parchment paper from 1 piece of dough. Brush the dough with a thin layer of olive oil. Spoon half of the peanut sauce with chicken on the dough. Top with ¾ cup of mozzarella cheese, scallions, carrots, and bean sprouts. Top with ¼ cup of mozzarella and the peanuts. Repeat this step to assemble the second pizza.

7. **Bake.** **STOP** Ask an adult to help put the pizzas in the oven. Set the timer for 10 minutes and bake until the crusts look golden and the cheese is melted and bubbly, 10 to 12 minutes. Remove the pizzas from the oven and top each one with the cilantro.

8. **Slice.** Allow the pizzas to cool for 2 to 3 minutes before slicing, and be careful when you take the first bite. Fresh pizza is delicious—but also very hot!

For Laughs!

What do you call a peanut in a space suit? *An astro-nut!*

GREEK PIZZA

PREP TIME: 20 minutes
COOK TIME: 10 minutes
MAKES: 1 (13-inch) pizza

TOOLS TO GATHER

Measuring spoons and cups

Grater

Pastry brush

Parchment paper

Rolling pin

Kid-safe knife

Sieve

Pizza pan, pizza stone, or baking sheet

Timer

MAKE IT YOUR OWN

Add cooked chicken breast or shrimp.

Think cool and crisp: juicy olives, salty feta cheese, and bright tomatoes. These Mediterranean flavors come together for a perfect pizza.

Extra-virgin olive oil, for brushing

½ batch **Super Simple Pizza Dough** (page 20) (use the other half for a different pizza or freeze it for later)

½ batch (¾ cup) **Super Easy Red Sauce** (page 33)

1 cup shredded **mozzarella cheese**

½ cup **black olives**, sliced

1 cup fresh **spinach** leaves

½ **red onion**

4 **sun-dried tomatoes** (about ½ cup), packed in oil

¼ cup crumbled **feta cheese**

1 teaspoon **salt**

½ teaspoon freshly ground **black pepper**

1. **Heat the oven.** Adjust the oven rack to the lowest position. Turn the oven on to 500°F.

2. **Prepare the dough.** Brush a piece of parchment paper with olive oil. Place the dough on the parchment paper and use a rolling pin to flatten it out into a 13-inch circle. Cover the dough with another piece of parchment paper and set it aside.

3. **Prepare the toppings.** Use a kid-safe knife to chop the spinach. **STOP** Ask an adult to help thinly slice the onion. Drain and chop the sun-dried tomatoes.

4. **Top the pizza.** Remove the top piece of parchment paper from the dough. Brush the dough with a thin layer of olive oil. Spread the red sauce evenly over the dough. Sprinkle with the mozzarella cheese. Top with the olives, spinach, red onion, sun-dried tomatoes, and feta cheese. Sprinkle with the salt and pepper.

5. **Bake.** (STOP) Ask an adult to help put the pizza in the oven. Set the timer for 8 minutes and bake until the crust is golden and the cheese is melted and bubbly, 8 to 10 minutes.

6. **Slice.** Allow the pizza to cool for 2 to 3 minutes before slicing, and be careful when you take the first bite. Fresh pizza is delicious—but also very hot!

TACO PIZZA

PREP TIME: 30 minutes
COOK TIME: 10 minutes
MAKES: 2 (13-inch) pizzas

TOOLS TO GATHER

Measuring spoons and cups

Grater

Kid-safe knife

Pastry brush

Parchment paper

Rolling pin

Large skillet

Wooden spoons

Small mixing bowl

2 pizza pans, 2 pizza stones, or baking sheets

Timer

MAKE IT YOUR OWN

Go vegetarian by skipping the meat.

Taco Tuesday just got a lot more fun . . . because now it's combined with Pizza Night! This is my favorite combination of toppings, but you can use your own favorite yummy taco fillings.

1 batch **Super Simple Pizza Dough** (page 20)

Extra-virgin olive oil, for brushing

1 pound **ground beef**

1 (1-ounce) package **taco seasoning** (or 1 teaspoon of cumin + ½ teaspoon each salt, oregano, and chili powder)

½ cup **water**

1 (15-ounce) can **refried beans**

¼ cup **salsa**

2 cups shredded **cheddar cheese**

¼ cup sliced **olives**

Toppings (each optional): **sour cream**, fresh **cilantro**, diced **tomatoes**, and **avocado**

1. **Heat the oven.** Adjust the oven racks to the lowest positions. Turn the oven on to 450°F.

2. **Prepare the dough.** If you haven't already cut the Super Simple Pizza Dough in half (see page 20), do it now using a kid-safe knife. Brush a piece of parchment paper with olive oil. Place 1 piece of dough on top of the parchment paper and use a rolling pin to flatten it out into a 13-inch circle. Cover the dough with another piece of parchment paper and set it aside. Repeat with the second piece of dough.

3. **Prepare the ground beef.** In a large skillet over medium heat, cook the ground beef, breaking it up with a wooden spoon, until it's browned, about 10 minutes. Drain the excess fat and add the taco seasoning and water to the skillet. Stir and simmer for about 5 minutes until the water has evaporated and the ground beef mixture looks thick.

4. **Mix the beans.** In a small mixing bowl, combine the refried beans and salsa, stirring it gently.

5. **Assemble the pizzas.** Remove the top piece of parchment paper from 1 dough circle. Brush the dough with a thin layer of olive oil. Spread half the refried beans mixture on the dough. Sprinkle with half the ground beef, half the cheese, and half the olives. Repeat this step to assemble the second pizza.

6. **Bake.** **STOP** Ask an adult to help put the pizzas in the oven. Set the timer for 8 minutes, and bake until the crusts are golden and the cheese is melted and bubbly, 8 to 10 minutes.

7. **Add the final toppings.** Either dollop sour cream and sprinkle chopped tomatoes, cilantro, and avocado on top of each slice, or let each person choose their own toppings.

CHICKEN TIKKA MASALA DEEP DISH PIZZA

PREP TIME: 20 minutes
COOK TIME: 34 minutes
MAKES: 1 (13-inch) pizza

TOOLS TO GATHER

Measuring spoons and cups

Grater

Cast iron skillet or 2-inch-deep pizza pan

Cutting board or clean counter space

Rolling pin

Baking sheet

Aluminum foil

Nonstick olive oil cooking spray

Kid-safe knife

Skillet

Large mixing bowl

Wooden spoon

Oven-safe tongs

Large spoon

Long metal spatula

Timer

DOUBLE IT

Want to make more than one pizza? Use a full batch of the Cornmeal Pizza Dough recipe (see page 24) and double the rest of the ingredients.

Hold the rice! Now your favorite buttery, smoky Indian dish comes on a pizza pie. You can even use pita or naan instead of dough—instead of baking the pizza, just broil it on high for 2 minutes.

For the dough

Butter, at room temperature, for greasing

Cornmeal, for dusting

½ batch **Cornmeal Pizza Dough** (page 24)

For the chicken

2 (8-ounce) boneless, skinless **chicken breasts**

¼ cup plain low-fat **yogurt**

½ teaspoon **garam masala**

½ teaspoon **salt**

For the sauce

1 tablespoon **extra-virgin olive oil**

1½ teaspoons **garam masala**

1 teaspoon peeled grated fresh **ginger**

3 **garlic** cloves, minced

1 (14.5-ounce) can unsalted diced **tomatoes**, drained

½ teaspoon **salt**

2 tablespoons **heavy (whipping) cream**

For the toppings

⅓ cup thinly sliced **red onion** (optional)

¾ cup shredded **mozzarella cheese**

2 tablespoons fresh **cilantro** leaves

1. **Heat the oven.** Adjust the oven racks to the middle and bottom positions. Turn the broiler on to high.

2. **Prepare the pan.** Butter the bottom and sides of a cast iron skillet or a 2-inch-deep round pizza pan.

3. **Prepare the dough.** Dust the work surface with a generous amount of cornmeal. Place the dough on the surface, then coat both sides with cornmeal. Flatten the dough a bit, then roll it out into a 17-inch circle (it should be larger than your skillet or pizza pan). Lift the dough and

carefully lower it onto the skillet. Lift the edges of the dough so that they sink into the corners of the skillet. Press all along the inside edge to make sure the dough is firmly tucked against the pan.

4. **Prepare the chicken.** Line a baking sheet with aluminum foil and spray the foil with cooking spray. Cut the chicken breasts in half lengthwise (so that they're long and skinny). Place the chicken pieces in a large mixing bowl. Add the yogurt and garam masala and stir to coat the chicken strips with the spice. Place the chicken strips on the prepared baking sheet. Sprinkle each strip with the salt. **STOP** Broil for 5 minutes. **STOP** Ask an adult to help flip the chicken, using oven-safe tongs, and then broil it for another 5 minutes. When the chicken is cool enough to handle, use a kid-safe knife to cut it into bite-size (about 1-inch) pieces.

5. **Adjust the oven temperature.** Turn the broiler off. Turn the oven on to 450°F.

6. **Make the sauce.** In a skillet over medium-high heat, heat the oil. Add the garam masala, ginger, and garlic. Cook for 1 minute. Stir in the tomatoes and simmer for 4 to 5 minutes. Add the salt and cream. Cook for 1 minute. Add the cut-up chicken and stir.

7. **Assemble the pizza.** Spoon the chicken tikka masala mixture onto the pizza dough. Top with the red onion (if using) and mozzarella cheese.

8. **Bake.** **STOP** Ask an adult to help put the pizza in the oven, on the middle rack. Set the timer for 15 minutes and bake the pizza. When the timer sounds, **STOP** ask an adult to help you rotate the skillet (turn it around), and bake the pizza for 12 minutes longer. When the cheese has melted and the crust looks golden, use a spatula to free the side of the crust from the skillet. Peek to check the bottom of the crust. Does it look golden, too? If not, **STOP** ask an adult to help move the skillet to the bottom rack in the oven and bake for 2 minutes longer. **STOP** Ask an adult to remove the skillet from the oven and let it cool for a couple minutes before asking an adult to help you transfer the pizza to a cutting board to slice.

9. **Finish.** Sprinkle the pizza with the fresh cilantro.

LEBANESE OLIVE PIZZA

PREP TIME: 20 minutes
COOK TIME: 10 minutes
MAKES: 1 (13-inch) pizza

TOOLS TO GATHER

Measuring cups and spoons

Kid-safe knife

Pastry brush

Parchment paper

Rolling pin

Cutting board or clean counter space

Pizza pan, pizza stone, or baking sheet

Timer

MAKE IT YOUR OWN

Use any combination of olives you like.

Traditionally a dish like this would use flatbread called *manakish*, or even pita bread, but our Super Simple Pizza Dough (see page 20) recipe works perfectly.

½ batch **Super Simple Pizza Dough** (page 20)

Extra-virgin olive oil, for brushing

½ batch (¾ cup) **Super Easy Red Sauce** (page 33)

1 cup shredded **mozzarella cheese**

½ cup crumbled **feta cheese**

1 cup **kalamata olives** (pitted and sliced)

½ teaspoon dried **oregano**

½ teaspoon dried **basil**

¼ teaspoon freshly ground **black pepper**

1. **Heat the oven.** Adjust the oven rack to the lowest position. Turn the oven on to 450°F.

2. **Prepare the dough.** If you haven't already cut the Super Simple Pizza Dough in half (see page 20), do it now using a kid-safe knife.

3. **Top the pizza.** Use the edges of the parchment paper to pick up the dough and transfer it to the pizza pan. Brush the dough with a thin layer of olive oil. Spread the red sauce evenly over the pizza dough. Sprinkle with the mozzarella cheese, feta cheese, olives, oregano, basil, and pepper.

4. **Bake.** STOP Ask an adult to help put the pizza in the oven. Set the timer for 8 minutes, and bake until the crust looks golden brown and the cheese is melted and bubbly, 8 to 10 minutes.

5. **Slice.** Allow the pizzas to cool for 2 to 3 minutes before slicing, and be careful when you take the first bite. Fresh pizza is delicious—but also very hot!

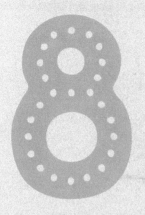

8

JUST FOR FUN

There's more to pizza than just cheese! From bacon and eggs to an explosion of chocolate, now you can eat pizza at any meal, from breakfast through dessert, whether you're eating at home or at school.

BACON & EGGS BREAKFAST PIZZA

PREP TIME: 20 minutes
COOK TIME: 24 minutes
MAKES: 1 (13-inch) pizza

TOOLS TO GATHER

Measuring cups and spoons

Kid-safe knife

Baking sheet, pizza pan, or pizza stone

Skillet

Metal spatula

Cutting board or clean counter space

Paper towels

Rolling pin

Pastry brush

Small bowl

Timer

HINT

Got a piece of eggshell in the bowl? Use a piece of the egg shell you cracked to scoop it out.

Pizza for breakfast? Yes, please! For this hearty start to the day, you can use turkey bacon, Canadian bacon, or any alternative you like.

1½ tablespoons **extra-virgin olive oil**, plus more for brushing

8 **bacon** slices, cut into 1½-inch pieces

Cornmeal, for dusting

½ batch **Super Simple Pizza Dough** (page 20)

8 ounces **mozzarella cheese**, thinly sliced

2 **garlic** cloves, minced

Kosher **salt**

Freshly ground **black pepper**

3 large **eggs**

2 tablespoons chopped fresh **parsley** leaves

1. **Preheat the oven.** Adjust the oven rack to the lowest position. Turn the oven on to 450°F. Lightly coat a baking sheet or pizza pan with olive oil.

2. **Cook the bacon.** Cook the bacon in a skillet over medium-high heat until it's crispy, about 4 minutes. Use a spatula to transfer the bacon to a plate lined with 2 paper towels.

3. **Roll out the dough.** Sprinkle a clean cutting board or counter with a handful of cornmeal. Use a rolling pin to flatten out the dough into a 13-inch circle. Transfer the dough to your prepared pizza pan.

4. **Add the toppings.** Using a pastry brush, gently coat the pizza dough with 1½ tablespoons olive oil. Top with the mozzarella cheese and bacon, leaving space for the eggs. Add the garlic, and season with salt and pepper.

5. **Bake the pizza.** STOP Ask an adult to help put the pizza in the oven. Set a timer for 10 minutes and bake the pizza.

6. **Add the eggs.** STOP Ask an adult to remove the pizza from the oven. Break 1 egg into a small bowl. Fish out any bits of shell, then quickly pour the egg into one of the spaces on the pizza. Repeat with the remaining 2 eggs. Set the timer for 8 minutes longer and bake the pizza until the egg whites have set and the crust looks golden brown, 8 to 10 minutes. For a nice fancy finish, add the chopped parsley.

7. **Slice.** Allow the pizza to cool for 2 to 3 minutes before slicing, and be careful when you take the first bite. Fresh pizza is delicious—but also very hot!

TRIPLE CHOCOLATE DESSERT PIZZA

PREP TIME: 15 minutes
COOK TIME: 20 minutes
MAKES: 1 (13-inch) pizza

TOOLS TO GATHER

Measuring cups and spoons

Baking sheet

Parchment paper

Small saucepan

Cutting board or clean counter space

Rolling pin

Pastry brush

Spoon or rubber spatula

Timer

MAKE IT YOUR OWN

Instead of chocolate-hazelnut spread, swap in peanut butter and chopped peanuts.

Not one, but three kinds of chocolate combine to make this the sweetest pizza you'll ever eat!

2 teaspoons **butter**

Cornmeal, for dusting

½ batch **Super Simple Pizza Dough** (page 20)

⅓ cup **chocolate-hazelnut spread**

½ cup **semisweet chocolate chips**

2 tablespoons **milk chocolate chips**

2 tablespoons **white chocolate chips**

1. **Preheat the oven and prep the pan.** Set the oven rack on the lowest position. Turn the oven on to 450°F. Line a large baking sheet with parchment paper.

2. **Melt the butter.** In a small saucepan on low heat, melt the butter. Set it aside.

3. **Roll out the dough.** Sprinkle a clean cutting board or counter with a handful of cornmeal. Use a rolling pin to flatten out the dough into a 13-inch circle. Transfer the dough to your prepared pan.

4. **Butter the dough.** Brush the dough with the melted butter.

5. **Bake the dough.** **STOP** Ask an adult to help put the pan in the oven. Set the timer for 18 minutes and bake until the pizza crust is crisp and pale golden brown, 18 to 20 minutes.

6. **Add the chocolate.** STOP Ask an adult to remove the pizza from the oven. It'll be very hot, so carefully spread the chocolate-hazelnut spread over the pizza with a spoon or rubber spatula, leaving a 1-inch uncovered border around the crust. Add all the chocolate chips to the pizza, STOP then ask an adult to return the pizza to the oven for 1 minute.

7. **Serve.** Cut the pizza into wedges and share.

HEARTS & STARS PIZZAS

PREP TIME: 20 minutes

COOK TIME: 6 minutes

MAKES: 8 to 10 small pizzas, depending on the size of cookie cutters

TOOLS TO GATHER

Measuring cups and spoons

Grater

Baking sheet(s)

Parchment paper

Kid-safe knife

Cutting board or clean counter space

Rolling pin

Large cookie cutters (3 to 4 inches in diameter)

Pastry brush

Large spoon

Timer

SWAP IT

Use Green Machine Pesto (page 36) in place of Super Easy Red Sauce.

Pizza doesn't have to be round! Use cookie cutters or a table knife to carve out special shapes. Bonus: A smaller shape will help the pizzas cook in less time.

1 batch **Super Simple Pizza Dough** (page 20)

2 tablespoons **extra-virgin olive oil**

1 batch (1½ cups) **Super Easy Red Sauce** (page 33)

2 cups shredded **mozzarella cheese**

1. **Preheat the oven and prep the pan(s).** Adjust the oven racks to the lowest positions. Turn the oven on to 400°F. Line 1 or 2 baking sheets with parchment paper.

2. **Arrange the pizza dough.** If you haven't already cut the Super Simple Pizza Dough in half (see page 20), do it now using a kid-safe knife. Either use your hands or a rolling pin to flatten 1 piece of dough until it's about ¼ inch thick—about the width of a chopstick. Repeat with the second piece of dough.

3. **Cut out shapes.** Use cookie cutters to make shapes out of the pizza dough. You should get 4 or 5 shapes out of each piece of dough. Arrange the mini pizzas on the prepared baking sheet(s).

4. **Add the sauce.** Use a pastry brush to coat the pizzas with the oil. Use a large spoon to ladle the red sauce onto each tiny pizza. Use the back of the spoon to spread the sauce evenly.

5. **Top with the cheese.** Sprinkle each pizza with shredded mozzarella cheese.

6. **Bake.** 🛑 Ask an adult to help put the pizzas in the oven. Set the timer for 4 minutes, and bake until the crusts looks golden brown and the cheese is melted and bubbly, 4 to 6 minutes, depending on the size and thickness of your pizzas.

LUNCHBOX PIZZA MUFFINS

PREP TIME: 30 minutes
COOK TIME: 25 minutes
MAKES: 12 pizza muffins

TOOLS TO GATHER

Measuring cups

12-cup muffin pan

Nonstick olive oil
cooking spray

Cutting board or clean
counter space

Rolling pin

Large spoon

Grater

Sharp knife

Timer

SWAP IT

Add any toppings you like:
pepperoni, olives, Canadian
bacon, pineapple . . .

Homemade pizza in your lunchbox never looked so cool!
Swirls of dough may remind you of a cinnamon roll, but
don't be fooled: This filling is made with tangy red sauce
and mozzarella cheese.

Cornmeal, for dusting

1 batch **Super Simple Pizza
Dough** (page 20)

1 batch (1½ cups) **Super
Easy Red Sauce** (page 33)
or **Green Machine Pesto**
(page 36)

2 cups **shredded
mozzarella** cheese

1. **Preheat the oven.** Position the rack in the middle of the
   oven. Turn the oven on to 400°F. Coat the cups of a muffin pan with cooking spray.

2. **Roll out the dough.** Sprinkle a clean cutting board or
   counter with a handful of cornmeal. Place the ball of
   dough on the cornmeal. Use a rolling pin to flatten out
   the dough into a large rectangle about ¼-inch thick (the
   width of a chopstick).

3. **Add the toppings.** Use a large spoon to ladle the sauce
   onto the pizza dough, and use the back of the spoon to
   spread it evenly. Sprinkle the mozzarella cheese on top.

4. **Make the pizza roll.** **STOP** Ask an adult to help you roll up
   the pizza (like cinnamon rolls or sushi) until you have a
   long log of pizza.

5. **Cut the roll into slices.** **STOP** Ask an adult to use a sharp
   knife to cut the pizza roll into slices about 2 inches thick.

6. **Bake.** Place 1 swirl inside each greased cup of the muffin pan. **STOP** Ask an adult to help put the pan in the oven. Set the timer for 20 minutes and bake until the cheese is melted and the dough is firm, 20 to 23 minutes.

7. **Store.** Allow the pizza muffins to cool completely before storing them in an airtight container for up to 5 days.

Did You Know?

Saturday night is the most popular night to eat pizza in America.

RAINBOW VEGGIE PIZZA

PREP TIME: 30 minutes
COOK TIME: 25 minutes
MAKES: 1 (13-inch) pizza

Measuring cups and spoons

Grater

Kid-safe knife

Pizza pan, pizza stone, or baking sheet

Paper towel (optional)

Cutting board or clean counter space

Rolling pin

Pastry brush

Timer

Red, yellow, green, and purple, this is the world's most colorful pizza. And with all those veggies, it's really good for you, too!

2 teaspoons **extra-virgin olive oil**, divided, plus more for greasing

Cornmeal, for dusting

½ batch **Super Simple Pizza Dough** (page 20)

½ batch (¾ cup) **Super Easy Red Sauce** (page 33)

½ cup shredded **mozzarella cheese**

4 cups colorful veggies (chopped **broccoli** or **green bell pepper**, chopped **orange bell pepper**, **corn kernels**, **halved grape tomatoes**, thinly sliced **purple potatoes**)

1 teaspoon **Italian seasoning**

¼ cup freshly grated **Parmesan cheese**

1. **Preheat the oven and prep the pan.** Adjust the oven rack to the lowest position. Turn the oven on to 400°F. While the oven warms up, drizzle a bit of olive oil into the pizza pan and use clean fingers (or a paper towel) to spread the oil evenly.

2. **Roll out the dough.** Sprinkle a clean cutting board or counter with a handful of cornmeal. Use a rolling pin to flatten out the dough into a 13-inch circle. Transfer the dough to the prepared pizza pan. Use a pastry brush to coat the dough with 1 teaspoon of olive oil.

3. **Prebake the dough.** **STOP** Ask an adult to help put the pan in the oven. Set the timer for 5 minutes and bake the dough. **STOP** Ask an adult to remove the pan from the oven.

4. **Add the toppings.** Drizzle the red sauce over the pizza dough and top with the mozzarella cheese. Arrange the vegetables in a circular or striped pattern by color. Drizzle the veggies with the remaining 1 teaspoon of olive oil and sprinkle with the Italian seasoning and Parmesan cheese.

5. **Bake again.** **STOP** Ask an adult to help put the pizza back in the oven. Set the timer for 15 minutes and bake until the vegetables are soft and the crust is golden, 15 to 20 minutes.

6. **Slice.** Allow the pizza to cool for 2 to 3 minutes before slicing, and be careful when you take the first bite. Fresh pizza is delicious—but also very hot!

For Laughs!

What vegetable do you throw away the outside, cook the inside, eat the outside, and throw away the inside? *Corn.*

MY ORIGINAL PIZZAS

Now that you're an experienced pizza baker, you can create any type of pizza you like! Use the following pages to make notes about your creations—you can even name your own pizza! You can also use these pages to make notes about how you changed one of the recipes in the book. The best part is that you can use the blank pizza to draw the pizza you made—or draw your fantasy pizza!

RECIPE NAME _____

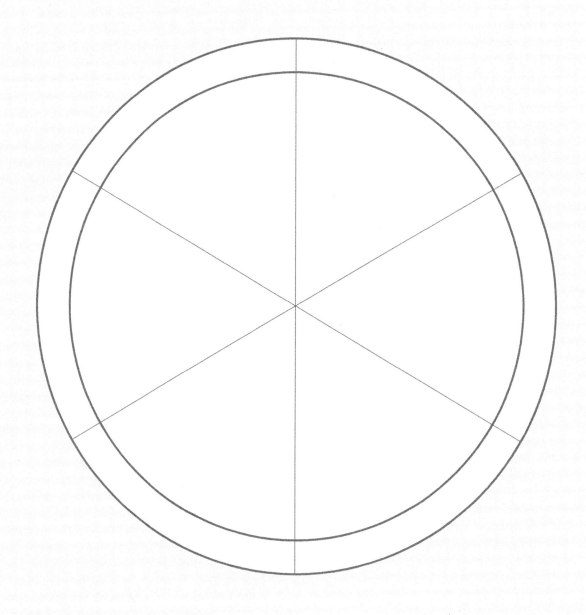

DOUGH _____

SAUCE _____

TOPPINGS _____

RECIPE NAME _____

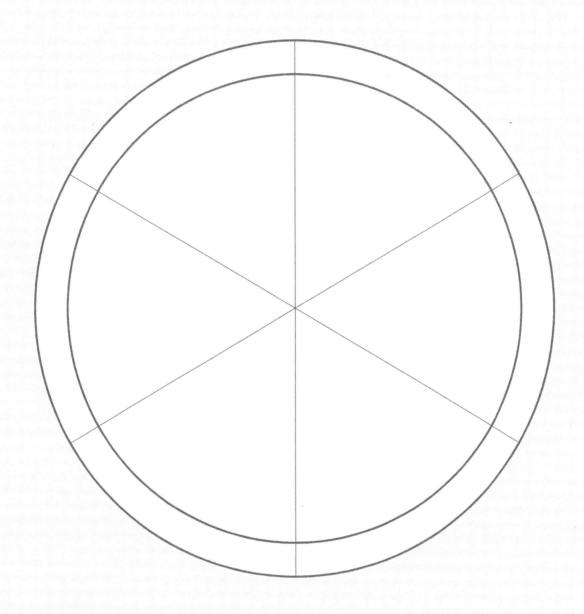

DOUGH _____

SAUCE _____

TOPPINGS _____

RECIPE NAME _____

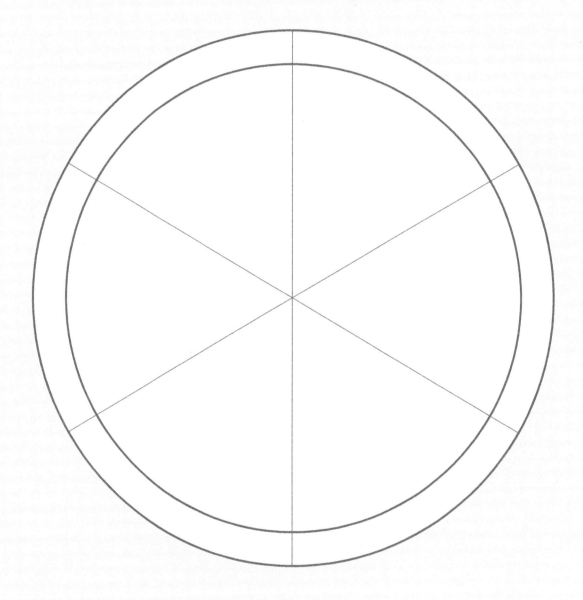

DOUGH _____

SAUCE _____

TOPPINGS _____

RECIPE NAME _____

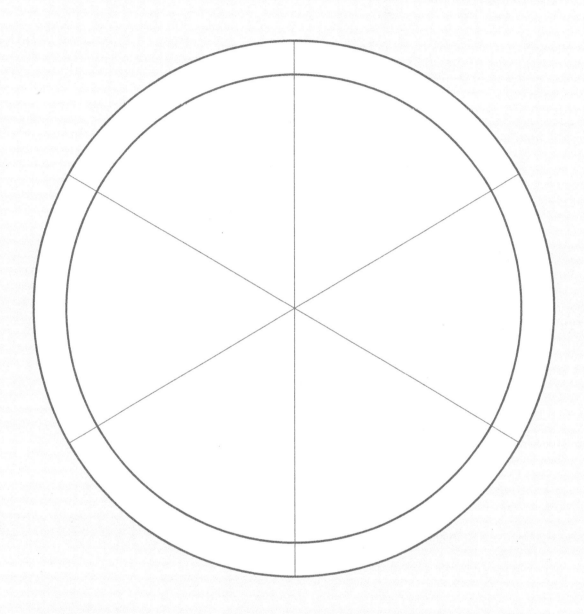

DOUGH _____

SAUCE _____

TOPPINGS _____

RECIPE NAME _____

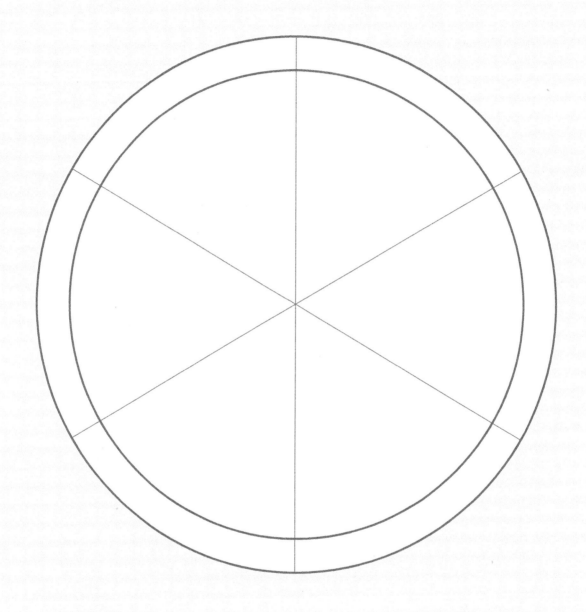

DOUGH _____

SAUCE _____

TOPPINGS _____

RECIPE NAME _____

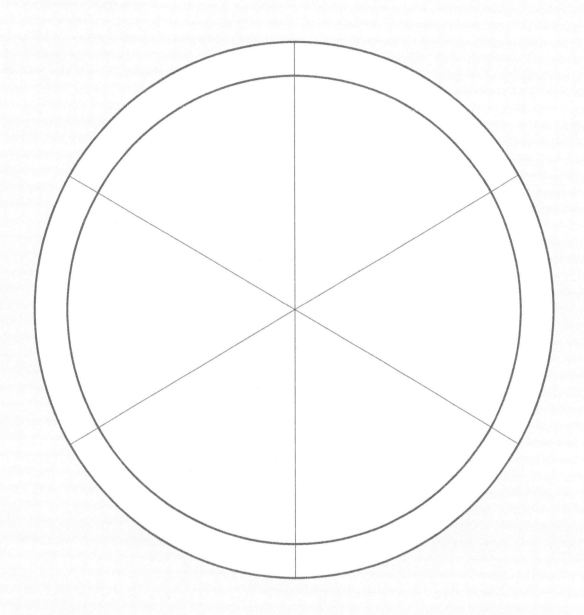

DOUGH _____

SAUCE _____

TOPPINGS _____

MEASUREMENTS CONVERSION TABLES

VOLUME EQUIVALENTS (LIQUID)

US STANDARD	US STANDARD (OUNCES)	METRIC (APPROXIMATE)
2 tablespoons	1 fl. oz.	30 mL
¼ cup	2 fl. oz.	60 mL
½ cup	4 fl. oz.	120 mL
1 cup	8 fl. oz.	240 mL
1½ cups	12 fl. oz.	355 mL
2 cups or 1 pint	16 fl. oz.	475 mL
4 cups or 1 quart	32 fl. oz.	1 L
1 gallon	128 fl. oz.	4 L

OVEN TEMPERATURES

FAHRENHEIT	CELSIUS (APPROXIMATE)
250°F	120°C
300°F	150°C
325°F	165°C
350°F	180°C
375°F	190°C
400°F	200°C
425°F	220°C
450°F	230°C

VOLUME EQUIVALENTS (DRY)

US STANDARD	METRIC (APPROXIMATE)
⅛ teaspoon	0.5 mL
¼ teaspoon	1 mL
½ teaspoon	2 mL
¾ teaspoon	4 mL
1 teaspoon	5 mL
1 tablespoon	15 mL
¼ cup	59 mL
⅓ cup	79 mL
½ cup	118 mL
⅔ cup	156 mL
¾ cup	177 mL
1 cup	235 mL
2 cups or 1 pint	475 mL
3 cups	700 mL
4 cups or 1 quart	1 L

WEIGHT EQUIVALENTS

US STANDARD	METRIC (APPROXIMATE)
½ ounce	15g
1 ounce	30g
2 ounces	60g
4 ounces	115g
8 ounces	225g
12 ounces	340g
16 ounces or 1 pound	455g

RECIPE INDEX

INDEX

ACKNOWLEDGMENTS

Thank you so much to the moms and dads who read Foodlets.com. Your support, comments, and suggestions have made writing for you my favorite job of all time.

To Paul, thank you for taking a job that took us to Italy, where our family first began.

To four people who truly guided us through our years in Rome with patience, curiosity (and best of all, the ability to speak Italian!): Giuseppe Micheletta, Molly Gage, Amy Flynn, and Dan Schiappacasse, you each introduced us to so many of our favorite things (that we still love to this day). I'll always be grateful.

To my little chefs: Phoebe, Estelle, George, and Violet, you're the best tasters—and recipe testers—I could ever hope for. I'm so proud to be your mama.

ABOUT THE AUTHOR

Charity Curley Mathews is a former executive at HGTV.com and MarthaStewart.com turned family food writer and speaker. The author of *Super Simple Baking for Kids* and *Kid Chef Junior Bakes*, she also blogs at Foodlets.com about parenting and kid-tested shortcut recipes full of fresh ingredients. She lives in North Carolina with her husband and four small kids on a tiny farm, currently home to 1 bunny, 2 naughty Lab rescues, 12 chickens, and 100,000 bees.

CPSIA information can be obtained
at www.ICGtesting.com
Printed in the USA
LVHW070020181219
640811LV00025B/780/P